D1147038

It's another great book from CGP...

There are only three ways to make sure you're fully prepared for the new Grade 9-1 GCSE Biology exams — practise, practise and practise.

That's why we've packed this brilliant CGP book with realistic exam-style questions for every topic, and we've got all the practicals covered too.

And since you'll be tested on a wide range of topics in the real exams, we've also included a section of mixed questions to keep you on your toes!

CGP — still the best! ☺

Our sole aim here at CGP is to produce the highest quality books — carefully written, immaculately presented and dangerously close to being funny.

Then we work our socks off to get them out to you — at the cheapest possible prices.

Contents

☑ Use the tick boxes to check off the topics you've completed.

Mixed Questions

Published by CGP

Editors:
Christopher Lindle, Chris McGarry, Ciara McGlade, Rachael Rogers, Camilla Simson

Contributors:
Bethan Parry, Alison Popperwell

With thanks to Phil Armstrong and Hayley Thompson for the proofreading.

ISBN: 978 1 78294 515 4

Based on the classic CGP style created by Richard Parsons.
www.cgpbooks.co.uk
Clipart from Corel®
Printed by Elanders Ltd, Newcastle upon Tyne

Mixed Questions

Published by CGP

Editors:
Christopher Lindle, Chris McGarry, Ciara McGlade, Rachael Rogers, Camilla Simson

Contributors:
Bethan Parry, Alison Popperwell

With thanks to Phil Armstrong and Hayley Thompson for the proofreading.

ISBN: 978 1 78294 515 4

Based on the classic CGP style created by Richard Parsons.
Clipart from Corel®
Printed by Elanders Ltd, Newcastle upon Tyne

Cells and Microscopy

Warm-Up

Use the words on the right to correctly fill in the gaps in the passage.
You don't have to use every word, but each word can only be used once.

Most ...*eukaryotic*... organisms are made up of many cells,

for example, ...*plants*... and ...*animals*... .

However, ...*prokaryotic*... organisms are single-celled and are also

...*smaller*... and simpler. They include ...*bacteria*... .

plants ~~bacteria~~
~~smaller~~ larger
animals
prokaryotic
eukaryotic ~~simpler~~

---

1 Which statement best describes the function of mitochondria?

    A   They are the site of photosynthesis.
    B   They are the site of respiration.
    C   They give support to the cell.
    D   They control the cell's activities.

Your answer *B*

[Total 1 mark]

---

2 Which of the following would you find embedded in a cell membrane?

    A   chromosomes
    B   chlorophyll
    C   plasmids
    D   receptor molecules

Your answer *D*

[Total 1 mark]

---

3 The diagram below shows a eukaryotic cell.

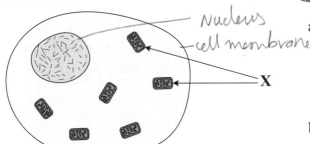

a) What name is given to the structures
     labelled **X** on the diagram?

     Mitochondria

[1]

b) Label the nucleus and cell membrane
     on the diagram.

[2]

c) Describe how the contents of the nucleus allow it to carry out its function.

*The nucleus contains DNA — an organism's genetic material —
the chemical instructions it needs to grow and develop.
in the form of chromosomes — controls the cells activities* *[2]*

[Total 5 marks]

4 The diagram below shows a prokaryotic cell.

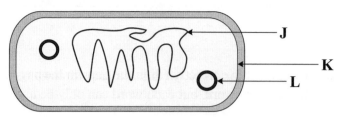

a) Name structures **J**, **K** and **L** shown on the diagram.

J ...... Chromosomonal DNA ......

K ...... Cell membrane ......

L ...... plasmids ......

[3]

b) Name **one** structure within a prokaryotic cell that contains genetic material.

...... plasmids ......

[1]

c) Describe **one** difference between bacterial cells (prokaryotic)
and animal cells (eukaryotic) other than their size.

...... most prokaryotes are simpler unicellular ......
...... eukaryotes are complex multicellular ......

[1]

[Total 5 marks]

5 Cells are observed using microscopes. (Grade 6-7)

a) A scientist uses a light microscope to view plant cells. The chloroplasts appear green.
Describe the function of chloroplasts and state why they appear green.

...... chloroplasts is where photosynthesis occurs. They contain ......
...... green pigment chlorophyll. ......

[2]

b) Electron microscopes can also be used to view plant cells.

i) How do magnification and resolution compare between electron and light microscopes?

...... electron - can ......

....

[2]

ii) How has electron microscopy increased our understanding of how plant cells work?

....

....

....

[2]

[Total 6 marks]

Topic B1 — Cell Level Systems

Light Microscopy

PRACTICAL

1 Which statement best describes when a stain might be used to view a sample of tissue?   Grade 4-6

    A   When the specimen is too thick for light to pass through.
    B   When the specimen is colourless.
    C   When there aren't many sub-cellular structures present in the cells.
    D   When a cover slip is not being used.

Your answer ☐

[Total 1 mark]

2 A student wants to use a light microscope to view a sample of cells that she has prepared. The diagram below shows a light microscope.   Grade 6-7

X

Y

Z

a) Give the name and function of the parts labelled **X**, **Y** and **Z** on the diagram.

    X ....

    Y ....

    Z ....
[3]

b) The individual steps taken when viewing a slide under a microscope are given below. Place the steps in order by writing the numbers **1-5** in the boxes.

	Use the coarse adjustment knob to bring the stage up to just below the objective lens.
	Select the lowest-powered objective lens.
	Use the fine adjustment knob to get a clear image of the specimen.
	Use the coarse adjustment knob to move the stage downwards to focus the image.
	Clip the slide onto the stage.

[2]

c) The student follows the steps above but finds that the image is too small to see the internal structures of the cells. Outline the steps she should take to get a bigger image of the cells using the light microscope.

....

....
[2]

[Total 7 marks]

Topic B1 — Cell Level Systems

More on Light Microscopy

1 A student observed a sample of cells under a microscope.

a) The student used an eyepiece lens with a magnification of ×10 and an objective lens with a magnification of ×40. What is the total magnification of the image?

answer = ...

[1]

b) By using the same eyepiece lens but a different objective lens the student changed the magnification of the image to ×100. Which objective lens did he use?

    A   ×10
    B   ×40
    C   ×100
    D   ×400

Your answer [A]

[1]

[Total 2 marks]

2 A student observed blood cells under a microscope. He takes a measurement of the width of one of the cells. The real width of the cell is 12 μm.

a) What is the real width of the cell in mm?
1 mm = 1000 μm. Give your answer in standard form.

$$10^{-3} = 110^{-6}$$
$$\frac{1}{10^3} = \frac{1}{10^6} \qquad \frac{10^6}{10^3} \qquad 3 \quad 1\mu = \frac{1}{10^3} \text{ mm}$$
$$\frac{12}{10}$$

answer = 1.2×10^{-2} mm

[2]

b) Another blood cell viewed under the microscope measured 0.0074 mm across. What is the width of the cell in nm?
1 mm = 1000 μm
1 μm = 1000 nm

$0.074 \mu m$

answer = ... nm

[2]

[Total 4 marks]

Exam Practice Tip

Don't panic if you have to give an answer in standard form. Just remember that the first number needs to be between 1 and 10. Then all you have to do to work out the power of 10 is count how many places the decimal point has moved. Don't forget to pop in a negative sign if the decimal point has moved to the right.

DNA

Draw lines to match each word or phrase on the left with the description on the right.

polymer   joins the two strands of DNA together

DNA   the genetic material of an organism

base pairing   the spiral shape of a DNA molecule

double helix   a long chain of repeating molecules

1 Which of the following shows a complementary base pair? **Grade 4-6**

   A   A-G
   B   G-C
   C   T-T
   D   C-T

A T
C G

Your answer [B]

[Total 1 mark]

2 Complete the following sentence about the structure of DNA. **Grade 4-6**

DNA is a polymer made up of monomers called:

   A   sugars
   B   amino acids
   C   nucleotides
   D   bases

Your answer [C]

[Total 1 mark]

3 The diagram below shows the structure of a DNA nucleotide. **Grade 6-7**

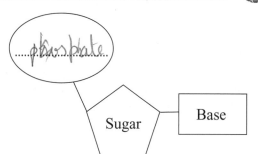

phosphate

Sugar   Base

a) Complete the missing label on the diagram.

[1]

b) Describe how DNA nucleotides can differ from one another.

The DNA C is the same. Only part that varies - Base.
Base is joined to sugar

[2]

[Total 3 marks]

Protein Synthesis

1   The diagram below represents a section of a DNA strand.   (Grade 4-6)

What is the maximum number of amino acids that could
be coded for by this section of DNA?

A   1

B   3

C   5

D   15

A C A G G T T T C A C C G T A

Your answer   B

[Total 1 mark]

2   Translation is a process that takes place during protein synthesis.   (Grade 4-6)

Which sentence best describes the process of translation?

A   Amino acids that match the sugars on the DNA are joined together in the correct order.

B   The mRNA unzips and the strands are used as templates to make DNA.

C   The mRNA strand is split up to form amino acids.

D   Amino acids that match the triplet codes on the mRNA are joined together in the right order.

Your answer   D

[Total 1 mark]

3   Protein synthesis begins in the nucleus of a cell. Describe the
stage of protein synthesis that takes place in the nucleus.   (Grade 6-7)

....

....

....

[Total 3 marks]

4   Haemoglobin is a protein that normally has a rounded shape. Its shape is important
for its role in carrying oxygen in red blood cells. In some people, one base in the
gene that codes for haemoglobin is replaced with a different one. Explain how this
alteration could lead to people having difficulty transporting oxygen in their blood.   (Grade 7-9)

....

....

....

....

....

[Total 3 marks]

Topic B1 — Cell Level Systems

Enzymes

1 Enzymes help to control chemical reactions in our cells.
Look at the table below. Which row best describes enzymes?

Grade
4-6

	are affected by pH	speed up reactions	get used up during reactions	all have the same shape
A	✓	✓		
B			✓	
C	✓	✓		✓
D		✓	✓	✓

Your answer ☐

[Total 1 mark]

2 The diagram shows an enzyme before and after it has been exposed to a high temperature.

Grade
6-7

X → high temperature →

before exposure   after exposure

a) Name the part of the enzyme labelled **X**.

....

[1]

b) Explain how the high temperature has affected the enzyme and how this will affect its activity.

....

....

....

....

[4]

[Total 5 marks]

3 Two different species of bacteria have slightly different versions of the same enzyme.
Enzyme **A** is from a species of bacteria found in a hot thermal vent and enzyme **B** is
from a species of bacteria found in soil. A scientist investigated the effect of temperature
on the rate of reaction for both enzymes. The results are shown on the graph below.

Grade
6-7

— line 1

···· line 2

Rate of Reaction

Temperature

Suggest which line represents enzyme **A**.
Give reasons for your answer.

....

....

....

....

[Total 3 marks]

Topic B1 — Cell Level Systems

4   A lipase is an enzyme that breaks down lipids into fatty acids and glycerol. The optimum
    pH of pancreatic lipase is approximately pH 8. The action of lipase results in the release
    of fatty acids, in the investigation this causes the pH of the test solution to decrease.

A student mixed pancreatic lipase solution with milk and recorded the change in the pH of the
solution. She took readings every two minutes for ten minutes. The results are shown in the
table below.

Time (minutes)	0	2	4	6	8	10
pH	9.2	8.8	8.5	8.0	7.6	7.3

a) Using the change in pH, calculate the mean rate of reaction during the ten minutes.

                              Mean rate of reaction = ... units of pH/minute
                                                                                      [2]

b) The student then investigated the effect of enzyme concentration on the action of lipase. At the
    end of her experiment she sketched the graph below, showing how the rate of reaction changed.

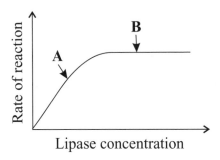

Explain what is happening at the points labelled **A** and **B** on the graph.

A ....

....

....

B ....

....

....
                                                                                      [4]

c) Explain **one** problem with using change in pH as a way of measuring the rate of the reaction.

....

....

....
                                                                                      [2]
                                                                          [Total 8 marks]

Exam Practice Tip
Lots of the questions in the exams will be based on experiments. Some of them will be testing your practical skills, but
some of them will just be getting you to apply your knowledge of a topic (e.g. how enzymes work) in a practical setting.

Topic B1 — Cell Level Systems

4   One method of making alcoholic beer involves breaking down barley grains to produce sugar. Yeast (a type of fungus) and water are later added to the sugar, and the mixture is left to allow the yeast to ferment. During the fermentation process, it is important that the mixture is held in a sealed container (e.g. a tank) to prevent air from entering.

a) Give another name for the type of respiration involved in making beer.

....

[1]

b) Write the word equation for the respiration reaction that takes place when making beer.

.... → .... + ...

[2]

c) Suggest why a tight seal on the container is important in the beer-making process.

....

....

....

[2]

[Total 5 marks]

PRACTICAL

5   A student was investigating the effect of exercise on his own breathing rate. He counted his number of breaths per minute before, during and after a period of exercise. He repeated his experiment three times. The results are shown in the table below.

	Breathing rate (number of breaths per minute)			
	Before exercise	During exercise	One minute after exercise	Five minutes after exercise
	11	16	15	12
	12	15	14	11
	11	15	14	12
Mean	11	15	14	

a) Calculate the mean breathing rate five minutes after exercise.

Mean = ... breaths per minute

[1]

b) Describe how the student's breathing rate changed during exercise compared to before exercise, as shown in the table. Explain why this change happened.

....

....

....

[3]

c) Give **one** other variable that the student could have measured which would have shown the same trend as breathing rate during exercise.

....

[1]

[Total 5 marks]

6 A scientist was measuring the effects of exercise on respiration. He asked a male volunteer to jog for 10 minutes on a treadmill. The speed of the treadmill was increased over the course of the 10 minutes, so that he was gradually working harder, until at the end he felt unable to do any more exercise. The graph below shows the oxygen consumption (the amount of oxygen used by the body per minute) of the man during the exercise.

Grade
7-9

a) Describe how oxygen consumption changed during the exercise.

....

....

[2]

b) In the final two minutes of the exercise, the man was respiring anaerobically.

i) Comment on the relative yields of ATP produced in aerobic and anaerobic respiration.

....

....

[1]

ii) Explain how the scientist may know when the man was respiring anaerobically by looking at the graph.

....

....

....

....

[2]

[Total 5 marks]

Exam Practice Tip

Don't be put off by any unfamiliar situations the examiners may throw at you — the facts of respiration will be the same, just don't go and mix up aerobic and anaerobic respiration. You don't want to end up throwing away easy marks.

Topic B1 — Cell Level Systems

Respiration Experiments

PRACTICAL

1   An experiment was set up using two sealed beakers, each with a carbon dioxide monitor attached. The set up is shown in the diagram below.

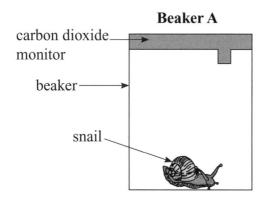
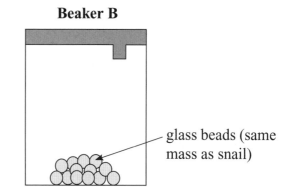

The percentage (%) of carbon dioxide in the air in both beakers was measured at the start of the experiment and again after 2 hours. The results are shown in the table below.

Time	% carbon dioxide in the air	
(hours)	Beaker A	Beaker B
0	0.04	0.04
2	0.10	0.04

a) Suggest **one** ethical consideration that must be taken into account during this experiment.

....

[1]

b) Describe and explain the results for **Beaker A**.

....

....

[1]

c) In the experiment, **Beaker B** was set up in the same way as **Beaker A** but with glass beads instead of a snail. Suggest why **Beaker B** is used in the experiment.

....

....

[1]

d) Suggest how the internal temperature of **Beaker A** would differ from that of **Beaker B** during the experiment. Explain your answer.

....

....

....

[2]

[Total 5 marks]

Topic B1 — Cell Level Systems

Biological Molecules

1 Which of the following molecules is a monomer?   Grade 4-6

    A   protein
    B   starch
    C   amino acid
    D   lipid

    Your answer ☐

[Total 1 mark]

2 Cell membranes contain structures called glycoproteins. As shown in the diagram below, glycoproteins are composed of both protein and carbohydrate.   Grade 4-6

The cell uses enzymes to regularly break down and rebuild glycoproteins.

a) State the type of monomer produced when the cell breaks down the carbohydrate portion of glycoproteins.

    ....

[1]

b) State the type of monomer the cell needs in order to rebuild the protein portion of glycoproteins.

    ....

[1]

[Total 2 marks]

3 Some bacterial species produce lipase (an enzyme that breaks down lipids). Two different species of bacteria were placed separately on an agar plate. The agar contained a lipid which made it cloudy. The plate was then left overnight. The results are shown in the diagram.   Grade 7-9

a) Bacteria that break down lipids are able to use the products of the reaction to transfer energy to the cell. Name the process the cells use to do this.

    ....

[1]

b) Use the diagram to suggest which species of bacteria contains lipase. Explain your answer.

    ....

    ....

    ....

[2]

c) Suggest why the pH on the surface of the clear zone might be lower than on the rest of the agar.

    ....

    ....

[2]

[Total 5 marks]

Testing for Biological Molecules PRACTICAL

Warm-Up

Draw lines to connect the tests on the left with the biological molecules that they identify.

Biuret test

Benedict's test

Emulsion test

Iodine test

Lipids

Starch

Proteins

Reducing and non-reducing sugars

1   A student is analysing the nutrient content of egg whites. *Grade 4-6*

a) Describe a test the student could do to find out if fat is present in a sample of the egg whites.

....

....

....

[4]

b) Describe how the student could test for protein in a sample of the egg whites.

....

....

....

[3]

[Total 7 marks]

2   A student was given test tubes containing the following glucose concentrations: 0 M, 0.02 M, 0.1 M, 1 M. The test tubes were not labelled and he was asked to perform tests to determine which test tube contained which glucose solution. *Grade 6-7*

a) Describe the test he could carry out to try and distinguish between the glucose solutions.

....

....

....

[3]

b) The table below shows the substance observed in the test tubes following his tests. Complete the table to show which glucose solution (0 M, 0.02 M, 0.1 M, 1 M) each test tube contained.

	Tube 1	Tube 2	Tube 3	Tube 4
substance observed	yellow precipitate	blue solution	red precipitate	green precipitate
glucose concentration (M)	....	....	....	....

[1]

[Total 4 marks]

Topic B1 — Cell Level Systems

Photosynthesis

Complete the following passage using words on the right. You do not need to use all the words.

Photosynthesis is carried out by organisms such as algae and

.... It uses energy transferred by

.... to produce ....

This energy is absorbed by subcellular structures called

....

mitochondria
glucose
green plants
fungi
chloroplasts
minerals
fructose
light

1 Photosynthesis is a chemical reaction, which allows photosynthetic organisms to generate their own food source.

Grade 4-6

a) Write the word equation for photosynthesis.

.... + ... → .... + ...

[2]

b) Photosynthesis is an endothermic reaction. This means that:

A energy is transferred from the environment during the reaction.
B energy is transferred to the surroundings during the reaction.
C energy is made during the reaction.
D energy is broken down during the reaction.

Your answer ☐

[1]

[Total 3 marks]

2 The sugar produced in photosynthesis can be broken down to transfer energy as part of respiration in a plant.

Grade 6-7

a) Give **one** other way in which a plant uses the sugar produced by photosynthesis.

....

[1]

b) Explain why photosynthesis is important for the majority of life on Earth.

....

....

....

....

[3]

[Total 4 marks]

Topic B1 — Cell Level Systems

The Rate of Photosynthesis

1 The distance of a plant from a light source affects the plant's rate of photosynthesis. **Grade 6-7**

a) Name the mathematical law that governs the relationship between light intensity and distance from a light source.

....

[1]

b) A plant is 40 cm away from a light source. The plant is moved so that it is 20 cm away from the same light source. Describe how the intensity of light reaching the plant will change.

....

[1]

[Total 2 marks]

2 The graph below shows how temperature affects the rate of photosynthesis in a green plant. **Grade 6-7**

a) Describe and explain the shape of the curve between points **A** and **B**.

....

....

....

....

[2]

b) Describe and explain the shape of the curve between points **B** and **C**.

....

....

....

....

....

[3]

[Total 5 marks]

Topic B1 — Cell Level Systems

Topic B2 — Scaling Up

The Cell Cycle and Mitosis

1 How many new cells are produced when a cell divides by mitosis? (Grade 4-6)

    A   2
    B   4
    C   8
    D   10

Your answer ☐

[Total 1 mark]

2 Which of these statements about the cell cycle is **true**? (Grade 6-7)

    A   Mitosis occurs twice during one turn of the cell cycle.
    B   The cell cycle involves several growth stages in addition to mitosis.
    C   Cells divide once by meiosis as well as once by mitosis during the cell cycle.
    D   The cell cycle only occurs in animals. Plants use a different process.

Your answer ☐

[Total 1 mark]

3 Mitosis can be split into several stages. (Grade 6-7)
The diagram below shows one of these stages.

a) Describe what is happening during the stage of mitosis shown in the diagram above.

....

....

[2]

b) Describe what happens to the cell after the stage of mitosis shown in the diagram above.

....

....

[2]

c) What must have happened to the cell's DNA before mitosis could take place?
Explain why this is necessary.

....

....

[2]

[Total 6 marks]

Cell Differentiation and Stem Cells

1 Stem cells are unspecialised cells that can become different types of specialised cells. **Grade 4-6**

a) Which of these is the name of the process by which a cell becomes specialised?

A   mutation
B   adaptation
C   functionalisation
D   differentiation

Your answer ☐

[1]

b) What is the benefit to plants and animals of having specialised cells?

....

[1]

[Total 2 marks]

2 Scientists can use stem cells to grow new cells, on which they can then test new drugs. **Grade 6-7**

a) Suggest **one** reason why scientists may prefer to use embryonic stem cells for research rather than adult stem cells.

....

....

[2]

b) In terms of their function, how do adult stem cells and embryonic stem cells differ?

....

....

[2]

[Total 4 marks]

3 The shoot tip of a plant can be used to grow a whole plant, through a process called micropropagation which is often used in scientific research. **Grade 7-9**

Using your knowledge of plant stem cells, explain how this process can generate whole plants.

....

....

....

....

[Total 3 marks]

 ☐ ☐ ☐

Diffusion, Active Transport and Osmosis

Warm-Up

The diagram on the right shows three cells. The carbon dioxide concentration inside each cell is shown. Draw arrows between the cells to show in which directions the carbon dioxide will diffuse.

carbon dioxide concentration = 0.2%	carbon dioxide concentration = 1.5%

carbon dioxide concentration = 3.0% ← cell

---

1 Osmosis is a form of diffusion. Complete the following definition of osmosis.

Osmosis is the net movement of .... molecules across

a partially permeable membrane from a region of ....

water potential to a region of .... water potential.

[Total 3 marks]

---

2 In which **one** of these scenarios is osmosis occurring?

A A plant is absorbing water from the soil.
B Sugar is being taken up into the blood from the gut.
C Water is evaporating from a leaf.
D Oxygen is entering the blood from the lungs.

Your answer ☐

[Total 1 mark]

---

3 Diffusion, osmosis and active transport all involve the movement of molecules. `Grade 6-7`

Draw arrows in the boxes underneath the diagram on the right to illustrate the net movement of the following:

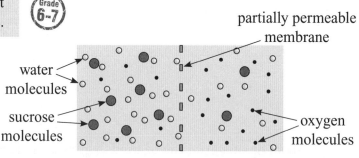

partially permeable membrane

water molecules

sucrose molecules

oxygen molecules

a) sucrose molecules moving by active transport:

[1]

b) water molecules moving by osmosis:

[1]

c) oxygen molecules moving by diffusion:

[1]

[Total 3 marks]

Topic B2 — Scaling Up

4 The cell membrane is important in controlling what substances can enter or leave a cell. The diagram below shows some molecules diffusing across a cell membrane. **Grade 6-7**

a) Describe the process of diffusion.

....

....

[2]

b) Which molecule shown in the diagram represents a protein?

A molecule **W**

B molecule **X**

C molecule **Y**

D molecule **Z**

Your answer ☐

cell membrane

W X Y Z

[1]

[Total 3 marks]

5 Amino acids are absorbed in the gut by active transport. The diagram below shows amino acids being absorbed into the bloodstream across the epithelial cells of the gut. **Grade 6-7**

mitochondria

epithelial cell

BLOODSTREAM

GUT

amino acids

a) Using the diagram above, explain why active transport is necessary for the absorption of amino acids into the bloodstream.

....

....

....

....

[3]

b) Explain why there are lots of mitochondria present in the epithelial cells of the gut.

....

....

[1]

[Total 4 marks]

Exam Practice Tip

Make sure that you've got diffusion, osmosis and active transport sorted — learn their definitions and make sure that you're crystal clear on the differences between them. If you don't bother I reckon you'll kick yourself after the exams...

Topic B2 — Scaling Up

PRACTICAL | # Investigating Osmosis

1   A student did an experiment to see the effect of different salt solutions on pieces of potato. He cut five equal-sized rectangular chips from a raw potato, each piece being 5 cm long, 1 cm wide and 1 cm deep. Each chip was placed in a test tube containing a different concentration of salt solution. The lengths of the chips were measured after one hour. The results are shown in the table below.

Test tube	1	2	3	4	5
Concentration of salt solution (%)	0	1	2	5	10
Length of potato chip after 1 hour (cm)	5.5	5.3	5.1	4.8	4.5

a) In which test tubes did the potato pieces increase in length?

   ....
   [1]

b) Explain what caused this increase in length.

   ....

   ....

   ....
   [2]

c) Calculate the percentage change in the length of the potato chip in test tube 5 in one hour.

   answer = ... %
   [2]

d) Plot the data from the table on the graph below. Draw a line of best fit through your points.

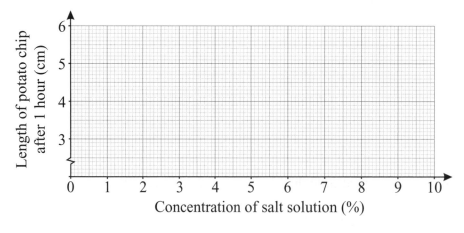

[2]

e) The student wanted to find a solution that would not cause the length of the chip to change. Use your graph to estimate what concentration of salt solution the student should try.

   ....
   [1]

   [Total 8 marks]

3 The roots of plants are covered in millions of root hair cells which are specialised for the exchange of water and mineral ions. *Grade 6-7*

a) Explain how root hair cells take up water from the soil.

....

....

....

....

[2]

b) The concentration of mineral ions is often higher in the plant than the soil.
Name the process by which the roots take up mineral ions.

....

[1]

[Total 3 marks]

4 The small intestine is where the products of digestion are absorbed into the blood. State and explain **two** ways in which the structure of the small intestine enables it to carry out its function effectively. *Grade 6-7*

....

....

....

....

....

....

[Total 4 marks]

5 Emphysema is a disease that weakens and breaks down the walls of the alveoli. Suggest why a person with emphysema may have a lower concentration of oxygen in their blood than a person who doesn't have the disease. *Grade 7-9*

....

....

....

....

[Total 3 marks]

Exam Practice Tip

It may seem obvious, but if you're asked to explain how the structure of something relates to its function, don't just dive straight in and rattle off what it looks like. You need to focus on the function and then pick out the individual structures that could help it to carry out that function. For each structure, make sure you give a clear explanation of how it helps.

Topic B2 — Scaling Up

The Circulatory System

Use the words on the right to correctly fill in the gaps in the passage.
You don't have to use every word, but each word can only be used once.

coronary

carbon dioxide

oxygen

mitochondria

pulmonary

cardiac

plasmids

The heart is made up of .... muscle. These muscle cells

contain lots of .... to provide the cells with ATP. They also

need their own blood supply to deliver nutrients and ....

Blood is supplied to the heart by the .... arteries.

1   Humans have a double circulatory system, in which the heart pumps blood around the body through a network of veins and arteries. The diagram below shows the human heart.

(Grade 6-7)

a) Name the parts of the heart labelled **X** and **Y**.

X: ....

Y: ....

[2]

b) Put the following stages in order to describe how blood flows through the right side of the heart by writing the numbers **1** to **5** in the boxes. The first one has been done for you.

	Blood is forced through a valve into the right ventricle.
	Blood enters the pulmonary artery, and heads towards the lungs.
	The atrium contracts.
	The ventricle contracts, forcing blood through a valve.
1	Deoxygenated blood flows into the right atrium from the vena cava.

[2]

c) Explain why the human circulatory system is described as a double circulatory system.

....

....

....

[3]

d) Explain the **benefits** to humans of having a double circulatory system.

....

....

....

....

[3]

[Total 10 marks]

The Blood Vessels

1 Blood is carried around the body in blood vessels.
   Different types of blood vessel perform different functions.

The diagrams below show three different types of blood vessel.

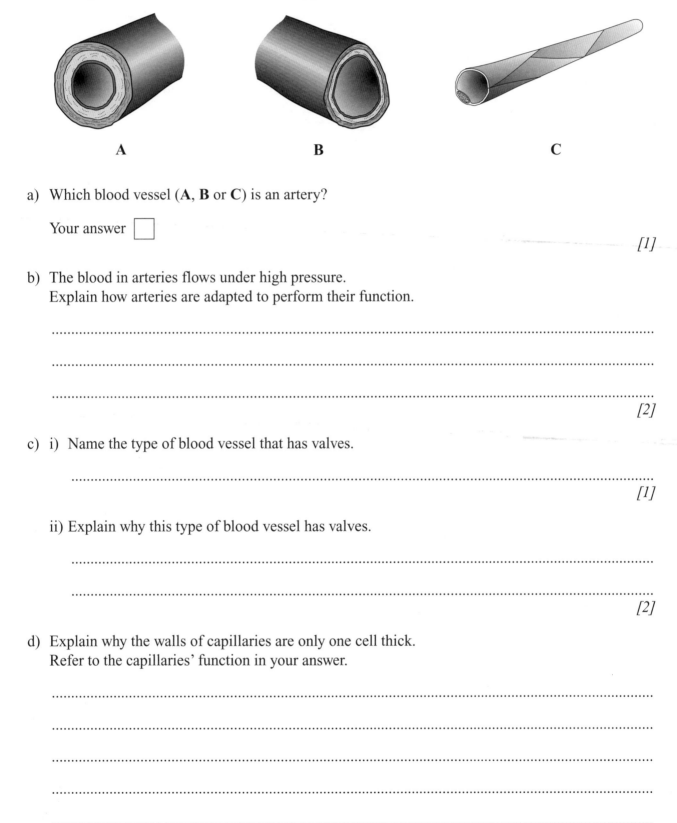

      A   B   C

a) Which blood vessel (**A**, **B** or **C**) is an artery?

Your answer ☐

[1]

b) The blood in arteries flows under high pressure.
    Explain how arteries are adapted to perform their function.

....

....

....

[2]

c) i) Name the type of blood vessel that has valves.

....

[1]

ii) Explain why this type of blood vessel has valves.

....

....

[2]

d) Explain why the walls of capillaries are only one cell thick.
    Refer to the capillaries' function in your answer.

....

....

....

....

....

[2]

[Total 8 marks]

 ☐ ☐ ☐

Topic B2 — Scaling Up

The Blood

1 Blood is made up of several different components. Grade 6-7

The components of blood can be separated by spinning them at high speed.
The diagram below shows a tube of blood that has been separated in this way.

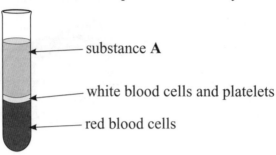

— substance **A**

— white blood cells and platelets

— red blood cells

a) Identify the substance labelled **A**.

....

[1]

b) Substance **A** transports the blood cells, as well as nutrients and other substances, around the body.
Give **three** examples of substances, other than cells, which are transported in substance **A**.

....

....

[3]

[Total 4 marks]

2 Red blood cells carry oxygen in the blood to other tissues in the body. Grade 7-9

a) Explain how the structure of red blood cells make them well adapted to their function.

....

....

....

....

[3]

b) Thalassaemia is a genetic condition which can cause people to have less haemoglobin than
normal in their red blood cells. One of the symptoms of this condition is tiredness. Suggest why
a decreased amount of haemoglobin in a person's red blood cells may result in tiredness.

....

....

....

....

[4]

[Total 7 marks]

Plant Transport Systems and Transpiration

Warm-Up

Use the words below to correctly fill in the gaps in the passage.
You don't have to use every word, but each word can only be used once.

perspiration   leaves   translocation stream   mineral ions   transpiration stream

roots   translocation   transpiration   sugars   evaporation   stem

The process by which water is moved up a plant is called .... It is

caused by the .... and diffusion of water from a plant's surface, most

often from the .... This causes a constant ....

to flow through the plant as more water is drawn up from the .... to

replace the lost water. Another process, called ...., is the transport of

.... and other food substances around the plant.

1   Plants have two separate types of transport vessel. They are shown in the diagrams below.   *(Grade 6-7)*

Vessel A   **Xylem vessel**

a) i) What type of vessel is vessel **A**?

    ....

    [1]

   ii) What is the function of vessel **A**?

    ....

    ....

    [1]

b) i) Describe the structure of xylem walls and what benefit they give to plants.

    ....

    ....

    [2]

   ii) Describe the involvement of xylem in transpiration.

    ....

    ....

    [1]

    [Total 5 marks]

Topic B2 — Scaling Up

More on Transpiration

1   The diagram below shows part of the surface of a leaf at high magnification.

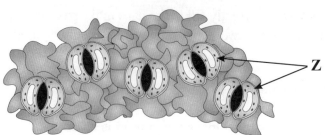

a)   Name the cells labelled **Z** in the diagram.

    ....

    [1]

b)   The cells labelled **Z** are responsible for the opening and closure of the stomata.
    Describe how these cells change in order for the stomata to close.

    ....

    [1]

c)   What is the purpose of stomata opening and closing?

    ....

    [1]

    [Total 3 marks]

2   The table below shows the diameter of eight open stomata.
    Four stomata were measured on two separate leaves (**A** and **B**).

	Diameter of stomata (μm)
Leaf A	25.2, 20.1, 18.7, 17.9
Leaf B	14.7, 12.8, 14.1, 13.2

a)   Calculate the mean stomatal diameter for each leaf.

                        Leaf **A** = ... μm   Leaf **B** = ... μm
    [2]

b)   Leaves **A** and **B** are from the same species. Suggest which leaf had its stomatal measurements
    taken at a **lower** light intensity. Explain your answer.

    ....

    ....

    ....

    ....

    [3]

    [Total 5 marks]

Investigating Transpiration [PRACTICAL]

1   A group of students were investigating the effect of air flow on the rate of transpiration. They set up a simple potometer as shown in the diagram below and kept the light intensity in the room constant.

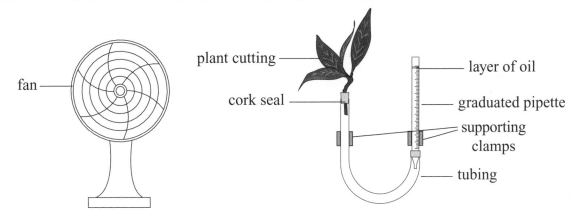

The students recorded the change in the volume of water in the pipette over 30 minutes, in normal conditions. They repeated this five times. They then carried out these steps with the fan turned on to simulate windy conditions. Their results are shown in the table below.

	Environmental condition	Repeat					Mean
		1	2	3	4	5	
Water uptake in 30 minutes (cm³)	Still Air	1.2	1.2	1.0	0.8	1.1	1.1
	Moving Air	2.0	1.8	2.3	1.9	1.7	1.9

a) Draw a bar chart to show the mean water uptake for still air and moving air.

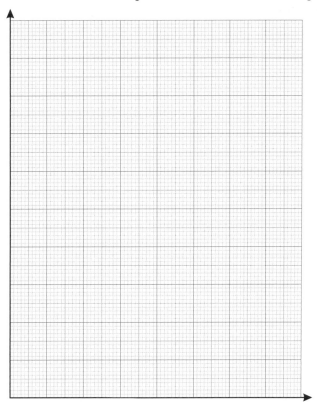

[3]

Topic B2 — Scaling Up

b) Calculate the range of the results for still air.

range = ... cm³

[1]

c) Describe the relationship between air flow around the plant and transpiration rate.

....

[1]

d) Explain the effect of air flow on the transpiration rate.

....

....

....

[2]

e) The rate of transpiration can be calculated using the formula:

$$\text{rate of transpiration} = \frac{\text{mean volume of water uptake}}{\text{time taken}}$$

Calculate the rate of transpiration for the plant in moving air. Give your answer in cm³/hr.

transpiration rate = ... cm³/hr

[2]

f) Another group of students carrying out the same experiment forgot about keeping the light intensity in the room constant. After the first repeat, one of the students turned on a light positioned near the apparatus. What effect do you think this would have on the water uptake in the remaining repeats? Give a reason for your answer.

....

....

[2]

g) Suggest how this experiment could be adapted to investigate the effect of changing the light intensity on the rate of transpiration.

....

....

....

[2]

[Total 13 marks]

Exam Practice Tip

Don't panic if you don't recognise the exact apparatus used in an exam question. As with many other bits of scientific kit, there are several different types of potometer. They all perform the same task, but some do it in a different way to others. If an exam question does use apparatus that you've not learnt about, you'll always be given all the info you need.

The Nervous System

Circle the examples that are reflex reactions.

Pedalling a bike.   The pupils widening in dim light.

Dropping a hot plate.   Running to catch a bus.   Writing a letter.

1 Which of the following sentences about reflex reactions is correct?

    A   Reflex reactions are slow and under conscious control.

    B   Reflex reactions are slow and automatic.

    C   Reflex reactions are rapid and automatic.

    D   Reflex reactions are rapid and under conscious control.

Your answer ☐

[Total 1 mark]

2 The diagram below shows part of the human nervous system.

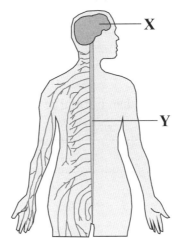

a) Name the structures labelled **X** and **Y** on the diagram.

    X ....

    Y ....

[2]

b) i) Which part of the nervous system do structures **X** and **Y** form?

    ....

[1]

ii) Describe the role of the part of the nervous system formed by structures **X** and **Y**.

    ....

    ....

[2]

[Total 5 marks]

3   Mohini put her finger near a candle flame. She quickly moved her hand away from it. The diagram below shows the reflex arc involved in this movement.

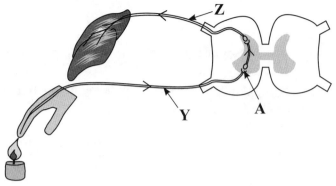

a) i) Name structures **Y** and **Z**.

Y ....

Z ....

[2]

ii) Structure **A** is the junction between two neurones. Name structure **A**.

....

[1]

b) In the reflex arc shown in the diagram above, state:

the stimulus ....

the effector ....

[2]

c) What makes reflex actions quicker than normal responses?

....

....

[1]

[Total 6 marks]

4   Information is passed along neurones as electrical impulses.

a) Name the long part of a neurone that impulses travel along.

....

[1]

b) Explain a structural feature of a neurone which can help speed up the transmission of impulses.

....

....

[2]

[Total 3 marks]

Exam Practice Tip

The pathway that nervous impulses take in a reflex arc is always the same — from receptor to effector. Learn the full details of the pathway involved and you'll be able to tackle any question on reflexes, even if it's a reflex you've not learnt.

Topic B3 — Organism Level Systems

5 Stimulants, such as caffeine, increase the rate at which nerve impulses travel. An investigation was carried out to assess the impact of different caffeinated drinks on reaction time.

The investigation involved measuring reaction time using a ruler drop test. In this test, a ruler is held above a student's outstretched hand by another person. The ruler is then dropped without warning and the student catches the ruler as quickly as possible. The distance down the ruler where the student caught it is used to calculate their reaction time in seconds (s).

Three different students (Students **1** to **3**) consumed a different caffeinated drink — each one contained a different amount of caffeine. Each student then undertook three ruler drop tests. The results are shown in the table below.

a) Calculate the mean reaction time for Student **2** and Student **3**.

	Reaction time (s)		
	Student 1	Student 2	Student 3
Test 1	0.09	0.16	0.20
Test 2	0.10	0.13	0.22
Test 3	0.43	0.15	0.19
Mean	0.21		

Student **2** = ... s

Student **3** = ... s

[2]

b) Identify the anomalous result in the table.

....

[1]

c) The students' reaction time without any caffeine was **not** measured. Explain why it should have been included in the investigation to assess the effect of each caffeinated drink.

....

....

....

[2]

d) Explain why the results of this investigation can't be used to **compare** the effect of the three different caffeinated drinks on reaction time.

....

....

[2]

e) An alternative version of the investigation was carried out. This time, the effect of a set quantity of caffeine on the reaction times of different individuals was investigated. Reaction times of three different students were measured, both before and after the consumption of caffeine. Give **three** variables that should have been controlled in this investigation.

....

....

....

[3]

[Total 10 marks]

Topic B3 — Organism Level Systems

The Eye

Use the words below to correctly label the diagram of the eye.

iris   pupil   suspensory ligaments   cornea   lens   optic nerve   retina   ciliary body

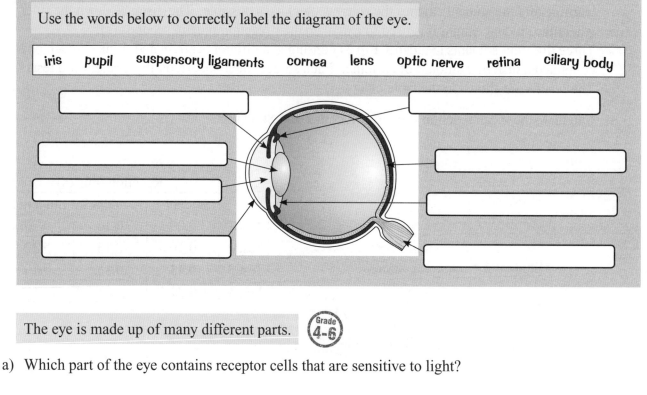

1 The eye is made up of many different parts. *Grade 4-6*

a) Which part of the eye contains receptor cells that are sensitive to light?

....

[1]

b) Describe the function of the iris.

....

[1]

[Total 2 marks]

2 Michael has been told by his optician that he is red-green colour blind. *Grade 4-6*

a) i) What is colour blindness?

....

[1]

ii) Give **one** way that colour blindness can be treated.

....

[1]

b) Michael wears glasses because he is short-sighted.
What does it mean when someone is short-sighted?

....

[1]

[Total 3 marks]

Exam Practice Tip

It's important to know the structure of the eye really well. If you do, it'll make understanding how the eye works and the problems that can affect the normal function of the eye (such as short-sightedness) easier to get your head around.

Topic B3 — Organism Level Systems

3 Keratoconus is a condition where the cornea gets thinner and changes shape. **(Grade 6-7)**

a) Describe the function of the cornea.

....

[1]

b) Suggest an explanation for why keratoconus affects a person's vision.

....

....

[2]

c) Suggest **one** way in which keratoconus might be corrected.

....

[1]

[Total 4 marks]

4 The picture below shows a man using glasses to correct his long-sightedness. **(Grade 7-9)**

a) i) Describe where light is brought into focus in the eye of a person who is long-sighted.

....

[1]

ii) Explain how long-sightedness can be treated with glasses.

....

....

[2]

b) In people with normal vision, explain how the shape of the lens changes to allow a person to see nearby objects clearly.

....

....

....

....

[4]

[Total 7 marks]

Topic B3 — Organism Level Systems

The Brain

1   The brain has different regions that carry out different functions.   Grade 4-6

   a) Which region of the brain is concerned with language?

      A   cerebellum
      B   cerebrum
      C   medulla
      D   hypothalamus

      Your answer ☐

[1]

   b) Name the region of the brain that controls unconscious activities.

      ....

[1]

   c) State **two** activities that take place in the human body which are not under our conscious control.

      ....

      ....

[2]

[Total 4 marks]

2   A hospital patient has suffered a serious head injury. Doctors are concerned that the patient's brain function might have been affected. The diagram below shows different regions of the brain.   Grade 6-7

   a) Doctors discover that the region labelled **D** has been damaged. What body function would this affect?

      ....   A ———

[1]

   b) After tests, the doctors confirm that the region of the brain controlling body temperature is undamaged. Which region (**A**, **B**, **C** or **D**) controls this function? Give the name of this region.

      Region ☐

      Name: ....

[2]

      B   C   D

   c) It can be difficult for doctors to treat problems with the brain and other parts of the nervous system. Describe **two** reasons why successful treatment can be difficult.

      ....

      ....

      ....

      ....

[2]

[Total 5 marks]

Hormones and Negative Feedback Systems

The graph below shows the change in the level of a hormone controlled by a negative feedback response over time.
Use the words on the right to fill in the labels on the graph.

normal   low   stimulated

inhibited   high

release of hormone ....

.... level of hormone detected

Blood hormone level

.... level of hormone

.... level of hormone detected

Time

release of hormone ....

---

1 Hormones are chemical messengers that affect the behaviour of their target cells. Explain how hormones reach their target cells and cause them to respond.

(Grade 6-7)

....

....

....

[Total 3 marks]

2 Thyroxine and adrenaline are hormones that are released in the body.

(Grade 6-7)

a) Which statement best describes the role of thyroxine in the body?

    A   It is involved in determining skin colour.

    B   It regulates the metabolic rate.

    C   It is produced in response to stress.

    D   It decreases liver function.

Your answer ☐

[1]

b) Where is adrenaline released from?

....

[1]

c) Give an example of a situation that might trigger adrenaline release and describe the effect this might have on the body.

....

....

....

[3]

[Total 5 marks]

Topic B3 — Organism Level Systems

Hormones in Reproduction

1 The release of sex hormones begins at puberty. **(Grade 4-6)**

a) What is the name of the main female hormone, produced in the ovaries?

....

[1]

b) i) Name the hormone that stimulates sperm production in men.

....

[1]

ii) Where in the male body is this hormone produced?

....

[1]

[Total 3 marks]

2 The diagram shows how the levels of four hormones change during the menstrual cycle. **(Grade 6-7)**

a) During which time period marked on the diagram (**A**, **B**, **C** or **D**) does menstruation occur?

....

[1]

b) Add an arrow (↑) to the *x*-axis of the diagram, to show the time at which ovulation occurs.

[1]

c) Before ovulation can occur, an egg must mature. Name the hormone that causes this.

....

[1]

d) Name the hormone marked **X** on the diagram and explain its roles in the menstrual cycle.

....

....

....

[3]

[Total 6 marks]

Topic B3 — Organism Level Systems

Hormones for Fertility and Contraception

1 A couple want to have children but the woman has not yet become pregnant. Blood tests have shown that she has a low level of follicle-stimulating hormone (FSH). She is treated with a fertility drug.

Grade 6-7

a) Explain why a low level of FSH may be preventing the woman from becoming pregnant.

....

....

[2]

b) In addition to FSH, which other hormone may the fertility drug contain to help the woman become pregnant?

....

[1]

[Total 3 marks]

2 The mini-pill is a method of oral contraception. It contains progesterone and needs to be taken around the same time every day.

Grade 6-7

a) Name **three** other types of contraceptive that use **only** progesterone.

....

....

[3]

b) Like the mini-pill, the combined pill also contains progesterone. Name the other hormone that the combined pill contains.

....

[1]

c) Many women who take the mini-pill don't ovulate.

i) Explain why taking the mini-pill may prevent ovulation.

....

....

[2]

ii) It's not only the effect on ovulation that makes the mini-pill an effective contraceptive. Explain **two** other ways in which the mini-pill can prevent pregnancy.

....

....

....

[2]

[Total 8 marks]

Exam Practice Tip

For this stuff to make sense it's important to have learnt the menstrual cycle and all the different hormones involved.

Topic B3 — Organism Level Systems

More on Contraception

Sort the methods of contraception into the correct columns in the table.

'natural' methods

condom   contraceptive injection

diaphragm   combined pill

intrauterine device (IUD)

mini-pill   sterilisation

contraceptive patch

Hormonal	Non-hormonal

1   Fertility can be controlled by non-hormonal methods of contraception.   Grade 6-7

a) Name a barrier method of contraception that can be used by women.

....
[1]

b) How do barrier methods of contraception prevent pregnancy?

....
[1]

c) Which form of non-hormonal contraception is the least effective?

....
[1]

d) Sterilisation is a permanent method of contraception that can be carried out on both men and women. Explain how sterilisation of men and women prevents pregnancy.

....

....
[2]

e) i) Explain how intrauterine devices prevent pregnancy.

....

....
[2]

ii) Give **two** advantages of the intrauterine device over the female condom.

....

....
[2]

[Total 9 marks]

Topic B3 — Organism Level Systems

Plant Growth Hormones

1 Two sets of cress seedlings were allowed to germinate under identical environmental conditions.

Set A

Set B ← light

When the newly germinated shoots were 3 cm tall, the two sets of seedlings were treated as follows:

- The cress seedlings in Set **A** received continuous all-round light.
- The cress seedlings in Set **B** were placed in a box with a slit in one side so that they received light from one side only.

The results are shown in the diagrams on the right.

a) Compare the growth of the seedlings in Set **A** with those in Set **B**.

....

....

[1]

b) Suggest **one** advantage to the plant of this response.

....

[1]

c) Auxin is a hormone that controls the growth of a plant in response to light. Explain the results for Set **B**. Refer to auxin in your answer.

....

....

....

[3]

[Total 5 marks]

2 A tropism is a growth pattern shown by plants in response to a stimulus.

a) i) What type of tropism is shown by a root growing towards gravity? ....

[1]

ii) Explain how auxin is involved in causing this tropism.

....

....

....

[3]

b) Explain how auxin causes shoots to be negatively gravitropic.

....

....

....

[3]

[Total 7 marks]

Topic B3 — Organism Level Systems

Uses of Plant Hormones

1 Plants produce hormones to coordinate and control a variety of processes. (Grade 4-6)

Which of the following processes does gibberellin initiate in plants?

A   gravitropic root growth

B   seed germination

C   fruit ripening

D   phototrophic shoot growth

Your answer ☐

[Total 1 mark]

2 Ethene is an example of a plant hormone. It stimulates leaf loss in some plants. (Grade 6-7)

a) Describe how ethene stimulates leaf loss.

....

....

[2]

b) Give **one** other role of ethene in plants.

....

[1]

[Total 3 marks]

3 Plant hormones are often used by commercial fruit and vegetable growers. (Grade 6-7)

Give **two** ways that gibberellin can be used by commercial plant growers.

1. ....

....

2. ....

....

[Total 2 marks]

4 A gardener wants to clone (create exact copies) of a plant in his garden. He takes (Grade 6-7)
a cutting of the plant and dips it into a powder containing a particular hormone.

a) Suggest which hormone the powder contains.

....

[1]

b) Suggest what the powder is for.

....

[1]

c) What other product might the gardener use in his garden that may contain this hormone?

....

[1]

[Total 3 marks]

Topic B3 — Organism Level Systems

 ☐   ☐   ☐

Homeostasis

1 Which of the following is **not** part of homeostasis? (Grade 4-6)

    A   responding to external conditions
    B   maintaining a constant internal environment
    C   allowing large fluctuations in internal conditions
    D   responding to internal conditions

Your answer [ ]

[Total 1 mark]

2 A person's skin temperature was measured over a 50 minute period. (Grade 6-7)

During that time, the person began exercising. They then returned to a resting state before the end of the investigation. The diagram on the right shows the change in the person's skin temperature over the 50 minutes.

(graph: Temperature (°C) on y-axis from 34.0 to 35.5, Time (minutes) on x-axis from 0 to 50)

a) Suggest the time at which the person began exercising.

....

[1]

b) Calculate the rate at which the temperature increased between 20 and 30 minutes.

Rate = ...°C/min
[2]

c) The hypothalamus acts as the body's thermostat.
Explain how the hypothalamus detects changes in a person's body temperature.

....

....

....

[2]

d) Give **two** changes that occur in the dermis when an increase in body temperature is detected.

....

....

....

[2]

[Total 7 marks]

Topic B3 — Organism Level Systems

Controlling Blood Sugar Level

1 The concentration of glucose in the blood is controlled by hormones. (Grade 4-6)

a) Which gland in the human body monitors and controls blood glucose concentration?

   A pancreas

   B pituitary gland

   C thyroid

   D testis

   Your answer ☐

   [1]

b) Which hormone is produced when blood glucose concentration becomes too high?

   ....

   [1]

c) What happens to excess glucose in the blood?

   ....

   ....

   [1]

   [Total 3 marks]

2 Diabetes exists in two different forms, Type 1 and Type 2. (Grade 6-7)

a) What causes Type 1 diabetes?

   ....

   [1]

b) What can happen if Type 1 diabetes is left untreated?

   ....

   [1]

c) Type 1 diabetes is treated with insulin therapy. This usually involves injecting insulin into the blood. Suggest **one** factor that might affect the amount of insulin injected by a patient.

   ....

   [1]

d) What causes Type 2 diabetes?

   ....

   [1]

e) Other than prescribing drugs, give **two** treatments recommended for Type 2 diabetes.

   ....

   ....

   [2]

f) Give a risk factor for Type 2 diabetes.

   ....

   [1]

   [Total 7 marks]

Topic B3 — Organism Level Systems

3 In an experiment, the blood glucose concentration of a person without diabetes was recorded at regular intervals in a 90 minute time period. Fifteen minutes into the experiment, a glucose drink was given. The graph below shows the results of the experiment.

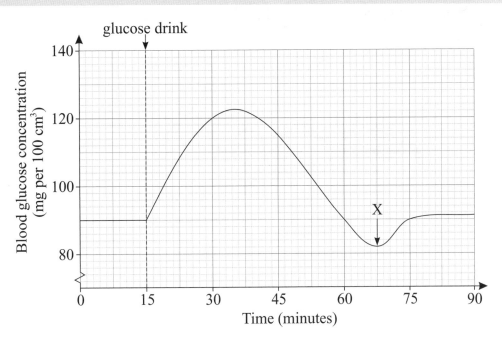

a) Explain what is happening to the blood glucose concentration between 15 and 60 minutes.

....

....

....

[3]

b) Name the hormone being released by the pancreas at point **X** on the graph.

....

[1]

c) Describe the effect that hormone **X** has on the blood glucose concentration.

....

[1]

d) Explain how hormone **X** causes this effect.

....

....

[1]

e) Suggest how the shape of the graph would differ if the person had Type 1 diabetes.

....

....

[1]

[Total 7 marks]

Exam Practice Tip

There are a few similar-sounding names when it comes to the control of blood glucose, so make sure you've got your head around which is which (and how to spell them). You won't get a mark if, for example, you write about 'glucogen'...

Topic B3 — Organism Level Systems

Controlling Water Content

1   The diagram below shows part of a kidney.

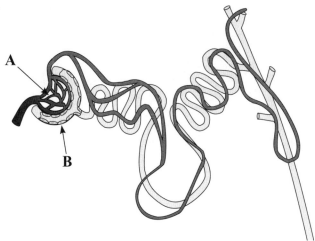

a) What is name of the entire structure shown in the diagram?

   ....

   [1]

b) Name **two** regions inside the kidney that this structure passes through.

   ....

   [2]

c) Name the parts labelled **A** and **B** in the diagram.

   A ....

   B ....

   [2]

   [Total 5 marks]

2   It is important that the water content of the body is balanced correctly. Imbalance between
     the water potential inside cells and the surrounding tissue fluid can damage cells.

a) Explain the effects on a cell if the tissue fluid surrounding it has a lower
    water potential than the fluid inside the cell.

   ....

   ....

   [2]

b) Explain how osmotic conditions would lead to cell lysis.

   ....

   ....

   ....

   [3]

   [Total 5 marks]

3 The kidneys play a vital role in controlling the water balance of the body.

This table shows the amount of water that is filtered by the kidneys in a healthy adult each day. It also shows the percentage that is reabsorbed into the blood.

	Amount filtered	Amount reabsorbed (%)
Water (dm³/day)	180	99.2

a) Calculate how much water is lost in the urine each day.

water lost = ... dm³/day

[3]

b) The volume of water in urine isn't always the same. Explain how the concentration of the urine is affected when the body loses water through sweating and doesn't replace it all.

....

....

....

....

[4]

[Total 7 marks]

4* The body is constantly monitoring and regulating its water content. Describe the body's response when the brain detects that the water content is too high. Include details of any hormones and structures involved.

....

....

....

....

....

....

....

....

....

....

[Total 6 marks]

Topic B3 — Organism Level Systems

The Carbon Cycle

1   The diagram shows part of the carbon cycle. The arrows indicate the transfer of carbon and carbon compounds within an ecosystem.

(Grade 6-7)

a) Using the diagram, give **one** abiotic component of the ecosystem that carbon cycles through.

    ....
                                                                    [1]

b) Name the process occurring at the point labelled **Y** on the diagram.

    ....

    ....
                                                                    [1]

c) Name the process by which plants obtain carbon from the air.

    ....

    ....
                                                                    [1]

d) Explain how fossil fuels can contribute carbon to the atmosphere.

    ....

    ....
                                                                    [1]

e) Describe what is happening at the point labelled **X** on the diagram.

    ....

    ....

    ....

    ....
                                                                    [2]
                                                          [Total 6 marks]

2   Many trees have fewer leaves in winter. Using your knowledge of the carbon cycle, suggest why this may contribute to an increase in the concentration of carbon dioxide in the atmosphere in winter.

(Grade 7-9)

    ....

    ....

    ....

    ....
                                                          [Total 2 marks]

Exam Practice Tip
There are lots of different ways that information about the carbon cycle can be shown, so don't be put off in the exam if you're presented with a cycle drawn differently to the way you're used to. Learn the cycle inside out and you'll be fine.

The Nitrogen Cycle and the Water Cycle

1 Fresh water is constantly recycled through the water cycle.   (Grade 4-6)

Complete the following sentences.

Heat from the Sun causes the .... of water from the land and sea.

Water is also transferred to the atmosphere from plants by the process of ....

As the warm water vapour rises, clouds form by the process of ....

Water falls from clouds in the form of rain, snow or hail, in a process known

as ....

[Total 4 marks]

2 All living things contain nitrogen. Nitrogen is constantly recycled in the nitrogen cycle.   (Grade 6-7)

a) Nitrogen is needed for making proteins for growth. Give **two** ways that atmospheric nitrogen is converted into nitrogen compounds that plants can use.

....

....

....

....

....

[2]

b) Nitrogen compounds are taken in by animals when they eat plants or other animals.
How are nitrogen compounds in animals returned to the soil?

....

....

....

....

[3]

[Total 5 marks]

3 Which of the following human activities might decrease the amount of nitrogen available to crops?   (Grade 6-7)

 A   Applying horse manure to the soil.
 B   Using nitrogen-based fertilisers on the soil.
 C   Over watering of the crops, causing the soil to become waterlogged.
 D   Planting legumes in amongst the crops.

Your answer ☐

[Total 1 mark]

Decomposition

Tick the boxes to show whether the following statements are **true** or **false**.

	true	false
Decomposers include bacteria and fungi.	☐	☐
Decomposers return proteins, carbohydrates and fats to the soil.	☐	☐
Most decomposers work best when there are low oxygen levels.	☐	☐
Decomposers can only respire anaerobically.	☐	☐
Decomposers contain enzymes which can be denatured at high temperatures.	☐	☐
The rate of decomposition is highest when there are really low moisture levels.	☐	☐

1   Felix investigated the decomposition of different food items. He placed tomatoes, bread and biscuits in three different places and left them for 10 days. He used the amount of mould present as a measure of decomposition. The amount of mould at the end of the 10 day period, in arbitrary units, is shown in the table below.

	Amount of mould present after 10 days (arbitrary units)		
	Fridge	In a cool place	Near a radiator
Tomatoes	2	7	15
Bread	0	3	12
Biscuits	0	0	0

a) Calculate the rate at which the bread placed near the radiator went mouldy.

Rate = ... units of mould/day

[1]

b) Felix noticed that the decomposition of tomatoes and bread was fastest near the radiator. Explain why this is the case.

....

....

....

[3]

c) Suggest why the biscuits didn't become mouldy during the 10 day period.

....

....

[2]

[Total 6 marks]

Ecosystems and Interactions Between Organisms

Warm-Up

Environmental factors can be abiotic or biotic. In each box below, write either the letter 'A' if the environmental factor is abiotic, or the letter 'B' if the factor is biotic.

☐ Moisture level   ☐ Number of predators   ☐ pH of soil

☐ Food availability   ☐ Temperature   ☐ Light intensity

---

1 Ecosystems are organised into different levels. *(Grade 4-6)*

Which of the following statements is the correct definition of a community?

A   A single organism.

B   All the organisms of different species living in a habitat.

C   All the organisms of one species in a habitat.

D   All the organisms living in a habitat along with all the non-living conditions.

Your answer ☐

[Total 1 mark]

---

2 Ants often live in the hollow thorns of a certain species of tree. The ants living in the trees feed on the trees' nectar. When herbivores try to graze on the trees, the ants bite them. Some ant species have also been shown to protect the trees from harmful bacteria. *(Grade 6-7)*

Which of the following statements best describes the relationship between the ants and the trees?

A   The ants are parasites because they depend entirely on the trees to survive.

B   The relationship is mutualistic because both the ants and the trees benefit from it.

C   The relationship is parasitic because the host is harmed and doesn't benefit from it.

D   The relationship is mutualistic because the trees depend on the ants to survive.

Your answer ☐

[Total 1 mark]

---

3 Prickly acacia is a tree species native to many African and Asian countries. It was introduced to Australia many years ago. It has invaded large areas of land in the warmer parts of the country. The trees grow best in areas with a high average temperature and where there is plenty of water, such as along rivers or on flood plains where there is seasonal flooding. *(Grade 6-7)*

a) Australia experienced particularly high rainfall in the 1950s and 1970s. Suggest how the prickly acacia population in Australia may have changed during these periods. Explain your answer.

....

....

[2]

b) Global temperature is thought to be increasing. What may happen to the distribution of prickly acacia in Australia over the next few decades? Explain your answer.

....

....

....

[2]

c) When prickly acacia invade an area it can negatively impact the population of various grasses in that area. Suggest why this might be the case.

....

....

[1]

[Total 5 marks]

4 Data suggests that since the 1960s roe deer populations in the UK have increased dramatically. The natural predators of roe deer include lynx, wolves and bears, but these are all now extinct in the UK. Roe deer usually live in woodland but they have more recently been observed in fields and scrub land.

Grade
7-9

a) i) Explain the biotic factors that may have contributed to the roe deer's expanding habitat.

....

....

....

....

[3]

ii) Some people are campaigning for the reintroduction of lynx in certain areas of the UK. What effect might this have on the population of roe deer in those areas?

....

....

[2]

b) Ticks are tiny animals that sometimes live on roe deer and feed on their blood. What name is given to this type of relationship?

....

[1]

[Total 6 marks]

Exam Practice Tip

Don't panic if you don't recognise the species in an exam question — the same stuff about competition for resources and the effects of biotic and abiotic factors will still apply. Read any information you're given carefully and apply it logically. If conditions are ideal for the organism and there's not much competition, populations will start to increase and vice versa.

Topic B4 — Community Level Systems

Food Chains and Food Webs

1   The diagram shows part of the food web in the Antarctic Ocean ecosystem.

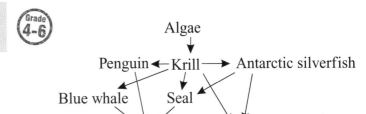

Which row in the table shows the correct trophic levels for these species?

	Producer	Primary Consumer	Secondary Consumer
A	Algae	Krill	Killer whale
B	Killer whale	Seal	Antarctic silverfish
C	Algae	Krill	Seal
D	Algae	Antarctic silverfish	Petrel

Your answer [ ]

[Total 1 mark]

2   The diagram shows some of the interactions between species in the rainforests of South America.

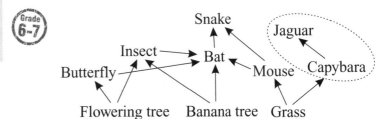

a) Describe what is being shown by the part of the diagram that has been circled.

....

....

[1]

b) What might happen to the populations of the following organisms if the banana trees are removed from the ecosystem? Explain your answers.

   i) Bats

   ....

   ....

   [1]

   ii) Mice

   ....

   ....

   [1]

   [Total 3 marks]

Topic B4 — Community Level Systems

Pyramids of Biomass and Number

The diagrams A-D shown below are pyramids of biomass. Which one represents a food chain with a producer, primary, secondary and tertiary consumers, and where the producer has the greatest biomass overall? Circle your answer.

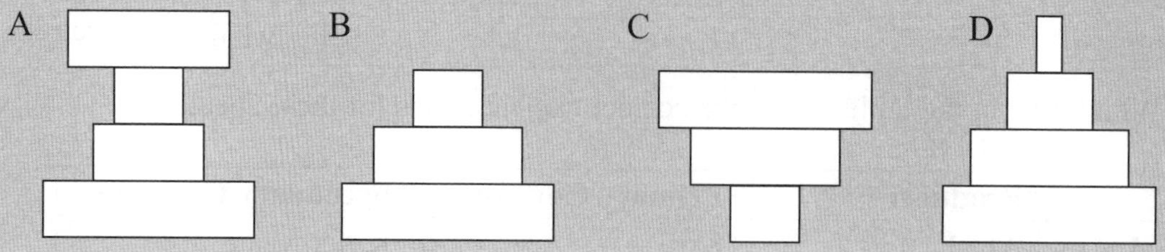

A   B   C   D

1 The diagram on the right shows a pyramid of biomass for part of an ecosystem in the African savannah.

(Grade 4-6)

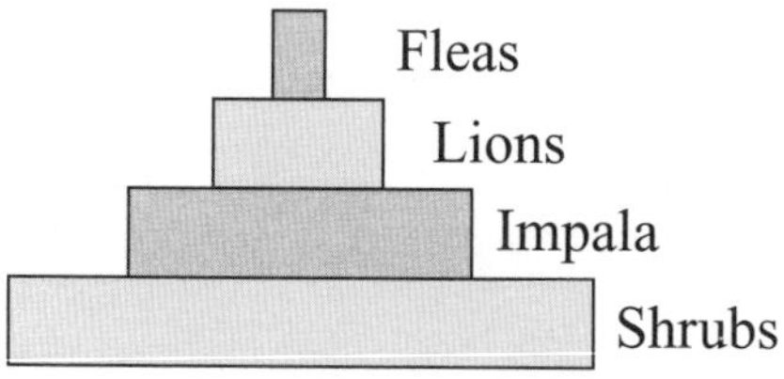

Fleas

Lions

Impala

Shrubs

a) Complete the sentences about the pyramid of biomass shown on the right.

Pyramids of biomass show the mass of .... at each trophic level

in a food chain. In this food chain, the .... are the producers because

they are shown at the .... of the pyramid. The food chain has

.... trophic levels. The .... are the

secondary consumers in this food chain. The pyramid is this shape because

.... is lost at each stage in the food chain.

[6]

b) Draw the food chain represented by this pyramid of biomass.

[1]

c) Suggest why the pyramid of numbers for this food chain may not be the same shape as the pyramid of biomass shown above.

....

....

....

[2]

[Total 9 marks]

Topic B4 — Community Level Systems

Biomass Transfer

1   A scientist is investigating the efficiency of a particular habitat. For one of the food chains in the habitat, she records the amount of biomass at each trophic level which is available to the next trophic level. Her results are shown in the table below.

Organism	Biomass available to next trophic level (arbitrary units)
Willow tree	312
Caterpillars	37
Hedgehogs	3.4
Hawks	0.3

a) How does the willow tree gain biomass?

   ....

   ....

   ....
                                                                                                        [2]

b) Calculate the efficiency of biomass transfer between the caterpillars and the hedgehogs.

                                          efficiency = ...% [1]

c) Suggest why the food chain only has four trophic levels.

   ....

   ....
                                                                                                        [1]
                                                                                            [Total 4 marks]

2   The diagram shows biomass transfer in a pond community. (Grade 6-7)

   Pondweed ⟶ Mayflies ⟶ Frogs ⟶

   Explain why not all of the biomass that the mayflies consume is available to the frogs.

   ....

   ....

   ....

   ....

   ....
                                                                                            [Total 3 marks]

Topic B4 — Community Level Systems

Genes and Variation

1   Genes are found on chromosomes.   (Grade 4-6)

What are chromosomes?

A   Enzymes used in the synthesis of proteins.
B   The bases that make up DNA.
C   Very long, coiled up molecules of DNA.
D   Proteins coded for by DNA.

Your answer ☐

[Total 1 mark]

2   Organisms have many different genes.   (Grade 4-6)

a) Explain the function of genes.

....

....

[2]

b) Explain the meaning of the term 'allele'.

....

....

[2]

[Total 4 marks]

3   Variation is the differences between individuals of the same species. It can be caused by differences in organisms' genotypes, interactions with the environment that organisms live in, or a combination of the two.   (Grade 6-7)

a) Describe the difference between the genotype and phenotype of an organism.

....

....

....

[2]

Many characteristics in humans show continuous variation.

b) Give an example of a characteristic which shows continuous variation.

....

[1]

c) Explain your answer to part b).

....

....

[1]

[Total 4 marks]

Genetic Variants

1 Mutations are rare events that can give rise to genetic variants. **Grade 6-7**

a) What is a mutation?

....

....

[1]

b) Which of the following statements is **true**?

    A   Most mutations have very little or no effect on the phenotype of an organism.

    B   All mutations affect the phenotype of an organism.

    C   Most mutations have a large effect on the phenotype of an organism.

    D   Mutations only affect non-coding DNA sequences.

Your answer ☐

[1]

[Total 2 marks]

2* Using your knowledge of mutations, explain how they can lead to a change in the phenotype of an organism. **Grade 7-9**

....

....

....

....

....

....

....

....

....

....

....

....

....

....

[Total 6 marks]

Topic B5 — Genes, Inheritance and Selection

Sexual Reproduction and Meiosis

1   In sexual reproduction, a male gamete fuses with a female gamete.

Which of the following statements is **true**?

   A   Gametes contain twice as many chromosomes as normal body cells.
   B   Gametes contain a quarter of the number of chromosomes in normal body cells.
   C   Gametes contain three times as many chromosomes as normal body cells.
   D   Gametes contain half the number of chromosomes in normal body cells.

Your answer ☐

[Total 1 mark]

2   Gametes are produced by meiosis.

Which of the following statements is **true**?

   A   Meiosis results in the production of two genetically identical gametes.
   B   Meiosis results in the production of four genetically identical gametes.
   C   Meiosis results in the production of two genetically different gametes.
   D   Meiosis results in the production of four genetically different gametes.

Your answer ☐

[Total 1 mark]

3   The diagram below shows two cells. The cell on the left shows
     a diploid cell with duplicated DNA about to undergo meiosis.

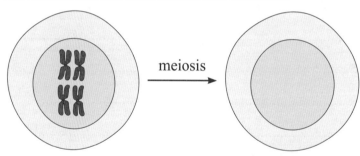

   a) In the cell on the right, sketch the number of chromosomes that would be present after meiosis.
                                                                                          [1]

   b) What term can be used to describe the number of chromosomes in the cell on the right?

....
                                                                                          [1]

   c) How many cell divisions take place in meiosis?

....
                                                                                          [1]

                                                                                   [Total 3 marks]

Exam Practice Tip

It's pretty easy to get mitosis and meiosis mixed up because someone decided to give them such similar names. Remember, when you're talking about the production of gametes for sexual reproduction, it's meiosis that you want.

Topic B5 — Genes, Inheritance and Selection   ☐   ☐   ☐

Comparing Asexual and Sexual Reproduction

For each of the following statements, circle whether the statement is **true** or **false**.

Asexual reproduction usually involves cell division by meiosis.	true /	false
Asexual reproduction results in genetically identical offspring.	true /	false
All animals are able to reproduce asexually.	true /	false

1   In some species of stick insect, females are able to lay eggs that hatch to produce offspring without being fertilised by a male.   *Grade 4-6*

a) What form of reproduction are the female stick insects carrying out? Explain your answer.

....

....

[2]

b) Explain **one** advantage and **one** disadvantage of stick insects reproducing in this way.

Advantage: ....

....

....

Disadvantage: ....

....

....

[2]

[Total 4 marks]

2   Peppermint plants can reproduce both sexually and asexually, although sexual reproduction takes longer to produce offspring.   *Grade 6-7*

Explain the benefit of peppermint plants continuing to reproduce sexually, despite it taking longer to produce offspring.

....

....

....

....

....

[Total 3 marks]

Topic B5 — Genes, Inheritance and Selection

Genetic Diagrams

Draw lines to match the words on the left to the correct definition on the right.

heterozygous

Having two alleles the same for a particular gene.

The combination of alleles an organism has.

allele

The characteristics an organism has.

Having two different alleles for a particular gene.

homozygous

A version of a gene.

1   Height in pea plants is controlled by a single gene. The allele for tall plants (T) is dominant over the allele for dwarf plants (t).   Grade 4-6

A student says that a pea plant must have the genotype TT to be tall.
Is the student correct? Explain your answer.

....

....

....

[Total 3 marks]

2   The picture below shows a tabby cat. Tabby cats have a distinctive banding pattern on their fur. The banding is controlled by a single gene. The allele for banding (B) is dominant over the allele for solid colour fur (b).   Grade 6-7

a) State the **two** possible genotypes for a tabby cat.

1. ....

2. ....

[2]

b) A heterozygous tabby cat breeds with a cat which is not a tabby.

Complete the genetic diagram to predict
the probability of one of the pair's offspring
being a tabby cat.

	....	....
....	....	....
....	....	....

probability of one of the offspring being a tabby = ...

[3]

[Total 5 marks]

Topic B5 — Genes, Inheritance and Selection

3 Hair length in dogs is mainly controlled by two alleles. Long hair is caused by a recessive allele (h) and short hair is caused by a dominant allele (H).

Grade 6-7

a) Give the genotype for a long-haired dog.

....

[1]

b) A homozygous dominant dog was crossed with a homozygous recessive dog.
They had 8 puppies. How many of those puppies would you expect to have long hair?
Construct a genetic diagram to explain your answer.

number of long-haired puppies = ...

[3]

c) A heterozygous dog was then crossed with a homozygous dominant dog.
They had 8 puppies. How many puppies would you expect to have short hair?
Construct a genetic diagram to explain your answer.

number of short-haired puppies = ...

[3]

[Total 7 marks]

4 Fruit flies can either have normal wings or small, deformed wings. The gene for normal wings is dominant. In an experiment, a scientist wanted to produce a population of fruit flies made up of 75% flies with normal wings and 25% flies with small, deformed wings.

Grade 7-9

Which of the following crosses would have the best chance of producing this population?

A Male NN × Female Nn
B Male NN × Female nn
C Male nn × Female Nn
D Male Nn × Female Nn

Your answer ☐

[Total 1 mark]

Topic B5 — Genes, Inheritance and Selection

Sex Chromosomes and The Work of Mendel

Circle the correct underlined words or phrases below so that the passage is correct.

Gregor Mendel was a monk who studied mathematics and natural history at the University of Vienna. He is best known for his early work on <u>speciation / evolution / genetics</u>, which he carried out in the <u>mid-1700s / mid-1800s / mid-1900s</u>. He proposed that characteristics were <u>passed on / lost / altered</u> from one generation to the next in "inherited factors".

1 Mendel's work is important for our understanding of inheritance. **(Grade 4-6)**

a) What organisms did Mendel use in his work?

....

[1]

b) What do we now call Mendel's "inherited factors"?

....

[1]

[Total 2 marks]

2 What is the chance that the offspring of human sexual reproduction will be male? **(Grade 4-6)**

A 60%
B 25%
C 50%
D 80%

Your answer ☐

[Total 1 mark]

3 Gender in humans is determined by the combination of the two sex chromosomes that an individual has. **(Grade 6-7)**

Which of the following statements is **true**?

A The presence of a Y chromosome results in male features.
B The presence of two X chromosomes results in male features.
C The presence of an X and a Y chromosome results in female features.
D The presence of two Y chromosomes results in female features.

Your answer ☐

[Total 1 mark]

Exam Practice Tip

Remember, if you're not sure exactly what the ratio of male to female offspring is, just draw a genetic diagram to work it out. Instead of putting different alleles in the diagram, just put the different sex chromosomes of each parent in.

Topic B5 — Genes, Inheritance and Selection

Classification

In classification, kingdoms can be subdivided into smaller groups. Write a number between 1 and 7 in each of the boxes below to put the groups in order of size, from largest (1) to smallest (7). The first one has been done for you.

☐ phylum   ☐ species   ☐ genus   ☐ order

[1] kingdom   ☐ family   ☐ class

1 The development of molecular phylogenetics has enabled us to discover new evolutionary relationships and clarify existing ones. The table below shows the percentage similarities between the DNA sequences of humans and a range of organisms.

Grade 4-6

Organism	A	B	C	D	E	F	G
% DNA sequence similarity to humans	18	87	44	26	92	96	54

a) Name the technique most likely used in molecular phylogenetics to gather this information.

....

[1]

b) Which organism in the table (**A - G**) is most closely related to humans?
Use information from the table to explain your answer.

....

....

[2]

[Total 3 marks]

2 There are many thousands of different organisms on the planet. Scientists use classification systems to classify these organisms.

Grade 4-6

a) What is classification?

....

....

[2]

b) Which of these statements about artificial classification systems is **true**?

A They use information about the common ancestors of organisms to classify them.
B They are the preferred method of classification for today's scientists.
C They rely on the use of detailed molecular techniques.
D They use observable features to group organisms together.

Your answer ☐

[1]

[Total 3 marks]

😐 ☐   🙂 ☐   😊 ☐

Evolution and Natural Selection

1   Scientists have discovered a species of wasp (species B) which they have evidence to suggest evolved from a closely related species (species A). The main difference between the two wasps is a difference in wing shape, which has been linked to variations in several alleles.

Grade 6-7

a) How do different alleles arise in a population?

....

[1]

b) The scientists think that the evolution of species B happened relatively quickly.
Give **one** factor which can affect the speed of evolution.

....

[1]

c) Describe how the scientists could test whether species A and B are truly separate species.

....

....

[1]

[Total 3 marks]

2   The photos below show two different hares. The hare on the left lives in a very cold climate. The hare on the right lives in a warm climate.

Grade 7-9

The hare on the right uses its large ears as a cooling mechanism. They allow lots of heat to leave the hare's body and regulate its temperature. The hare on the left has smaller ears.

Suggest how the species of hare on the left evolved to have smaller ears than hares that live in warmer climates.

....

....

....

....

....

....

....

....

[Total 5 marks]

Topic B5 — Genes, Inheritance and Selection

Evidence for Evolution

1 There is lots of good evidence for evolution. **Grade 6-7**

a) Fossils are a source of evidence for evolution. What is a fossil?

....

....

[1]

The diagram below shows the bone structure of a modern human foot and incomplete fossils of the feet of two ancient ancestors of modern humans.

Fossil A   Fossil B   Human foot

b) Suggest the correct chronological order of the bone structures from the oldest to the most recent.

....

[1]

c) Explain how arranging fossils in chronological order can provide evidence for evolution.

....

....

[2]

d) Another source of evidence for evolution is the ability of bacteria to evolve and become resistant to antibiotics. The process occurs rapidly, so scientists are able to monitor the evolution as it is occurring. Explain how the evolution of antibiotic resistance occurs in bacteria.

....

....

....

....

....

....

....

....

....

[5]

[Total 9 marks]

Darwin and Wallace

1 Charles Darwin and Alfred Russel Wallace developed a theory of evolution. (Grade 4-6)

   a) They proposed that evolution took place by one specific process.
   What is the name of that process?

   A   Natural selection

   B   Normal variation

   C   Normal selection

   D   Natural variation

   Your answer ☐

   [1]

   b) What was the name of the book written by Darwin about the theory of evolution?

   ....

   [1]

   c) Wallace observed that some species used warning colours to deter predators.
   Suggest how this supports Darwin and Wallace's theory of evolution.

   ....

   ....

   [2]

   [Total 4 marks]

2 Darwin and Wallace's theory of evolution widely influences modern biology. It's considered today in conservation efforts such as seedbanks, which are used to store plant seeds. (Grade 7-9)

   a) Explain how seedbanks can help to preserve biodiversity.

   ....

   ....

   ....

   [2]

   b) Seedbanks sometimes store the seeds of several individuals of the same species of plant.
   Suggest how this practice could be beneficial to the preservation of endangered plants in the wild.

   ....

   ....

   ....

   ....

   ....

   [2]

   [Total 4 marks]

Topic B5 — Genes, Inheritance and Selection

Investigating Distribution and Abundance

1   Which piece of equipment would be best for sampling the distribution of a species of grass?   *(Grade 4-6)*

    A   pooter
    B   quadrat
    C   sweep net
    D   pitfall trap

Your answer ☐

[Total 1 mark]

PRACTICAL

2   A group of students investigated the distribution and abundance of organisms in a local park.   *(Grade 6-7)*

a) What is meant by the term distribution?

....

[1]

b) One area of the park contains long grass. The students counted the number of individuals
of three different flying insect species in five sample areas of the long grass.
Their results are shown in the table below.

	Number of individuals counted				
	Sample area				
Organism	1	2	3	4	5
A	4	10	3	8	6
B	5	2	7	8	1
C	9	6	8	4	6

i) Suggest a piece of equipment they could have used to collect the organisms.

....

[1]

ii) Based on their results, which organism was the most abundant in the long grass?
Give a reason for your answer.

....

....

[1]

c) In a different area of the park, the students collected ground insects using a pooter.
Describe how a pooter could be used to compare insects in two sample areas.

....

....

....

....

[3]

[Total 6 marks]

PRACTICAL

3   Rebecca used a 0.5 m² quadrat to investigate the number of buttercups growing in a field. She counted the number of buttercups in the quadrat in ten randomly selected places. The table below shows her results.

Quadrat Number	Number of buttercups
1	15
2	13
3	16
4	23
5	26
6	23
7	13
8	12
9	16
10	13

a) i) Why is it important that the quadrats were placed randomly in the field?

....

[1]

ii) Describe a method that could have been used to randomly place the quadrats.

....

[1]

b) What is the modal number of buttercups in a quadrat in the table?

answer = ... buttercups

[1]

c) What is the median number of buttercups in the table?

answer = ... buttercups

[1]

d) Calculate the mean number of buttercups per 0.5 m² quadrat.

answer = ... buttercups per 0.5 m²

[1]

e) The total area of the field was 1750 m².
Estimate the number of buttercups in the whole of the field.

answer = ... buttercups

[3]

[Total 8 marks]

Topic B6 — Global Challenges

Using Keys and Factors Affecting Distribution

1   Samantha is using a key to identify some butterflies based on
     the markings on their wings. Part of the key is shown below.

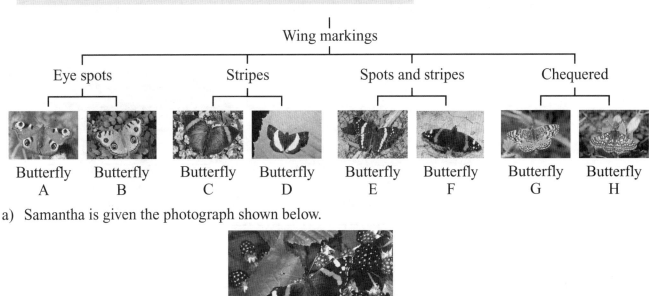

Wing markings

Eye spots   Stripes   Spots and stripes   Chequered

Butterfly   Butterfly   Butterfly   Butterfly   Butterfly   Butterfly   Butterfly   Butterfly
   A   B   C   D   E   F   G   H

a) Samantha is given the photograph shown below.

   i) Using the key, describe the wing markings shown on the butterfly in the photograph.

   ....

                                                                                                        [1]

   ii) Samantha uses the key to identify the butterfly species in the photograph — it is a Red Admiral
       butterfly. Which of the butterflies in the key is a Red Admiral butterfly?

   ....

                                                                                                        [1]

b) Samantha is using the key to try and identify another butterfly. The butterfly has chequered
    wing markings but she can't work out if it is butterfly **G** or **H**, as they look very similar.
    Suggest **two** things that could help Samantha make a definite identification.

   ....

   ....

                                                                                                        [2]
                                                                                          [Total 4 marks]

2   Students are investigating the distribution of different plant species
     using quadrats, in an area where soil pH varies considerably.

     Explain why the students may want to measure the soil pH at the site where each quadrat is placed.

   ....

   ....

   ....

                                                                                          [Total 2 marks]

                                        Topic B6 — Global Challenges

Using Transects

1 A transect was carried out from the edge of a small pond, across a grassy field and into a woodland. The distributions of four species of plant were recorded along the transect, along with the soil moisture and light levels. The diagram below shows the results.

Key
🌼 dandelion
🌼 daisy
🌾 short grass   🌿 long grass

pond   zone A   zone B   zone C   woodland

soil moisture level: high ——————————→ low
light level: high ——————————→ low

a) The grassy field is split up into three zones — **A**, **B** and **C**.
   In the diagram, which zones contained only **one** species of plant?

   ....
   [1]

b) Which of the four species of plant can grow in soils with both a high and low level of moisture, and at both low and high light intensities?

   ....
   [1]

c) Suggest **two** reasons why long grass, daisies and dandelions all grow in **zone A**.

   ....

   ....
   [2]

d) Children often play football on one zone of the grassy field. The trampling that occurs here makes it difficult for plants to become established. Suggest which zone might be used to play football. Explain your answer.

   ....

   ....
   [2]

e) A transect can also be used to determine the abundance of species in an ecosystem.
   Explain how this transect could be used to determine the abundance of the four plant species.

   ....

   ....

   ....
   [2]

   [Total 8 marks]

Human Impacts on Ecosystems

1   Ferrets were introduced into New Zealand in the 1800s. There are now many ferrets living in a variety of different habitats across New Zealand. They can disrupt an ecosystem by feeding on native species.

Which human activity is likely to have a **positive** impact on biodiversity in the ecosystems in which the ferrets live?

   A   Clearing large areas of the habitats in which the ferrets live.
   B   Setting out poisoned food sources across the habitat.
   C   Setting traps that will catch ferrets but not other types of animal.
   D   Removing the native species which the ferrets feed on.

Your answer ☐

[Total 1 mark]

2   Chester Zoo is home to around 500 different animal species. Many of these species are endangered in the wild.

a) Explain how keeping endangered animals in a zoo can help to protect global biodiversity.

....

....

....

[2]

b) Chester Zoo also has a nature reserve on site. The nature reserve has designated pathways from which visitors can view local wildlife. Describe how the nature reserve protects local biodiversity.

....

[1]

[Total 3 marks]

3*   Explain, with reference to land use and hunting, how an increasing human population can have a negative impact on global biodiversity.

....

....

....

....

....

....

....

....

....

[Total 6 marks]

Topic B6 — Global Challenges

Maintaining Biodiversity

1 The Ngorongoro Conservation Area is a large protected area in Africa. The authority that manages it helps to protect biodiversity in the area as well as encourage ecotourism.

Grade 6-7

a) i) What is meant by the term ecotourism?

....

....

[2]

ii) How will ecotourism in the Ngorongoro Conservation Area help the local human population?

....

[1]

b) Apart from ecotourism, give **one** benefit to humans of places like the Ngorongoro Conservation Area, which help to protect ecosystems.

....

[1]

[Total 4 marks]

2 Fishing practices are leading to a decrease in many fish populations all over the world. Bluefin tuna is a species of fish that is now much rarer than it was in the 1960s, due to overfishing. International organisations have since set a limit on the number of bluefin tuna that can be caught within a given period of time.

Grade 6-7

a) Give **one** reason why controlling the fishing of bluefin tuna may be beneficial to humans.

....

....

[1]

b) Many bluefin tuna live in shoals which migrate through international waters that do not belong to any specific country. This means that fishing vessels from many different countries fish for bluefin tuna. Suggest **two** reasons why this might make it difficult to reduce the number of bluefin tuna caught by humans.

....

....

....

....

[2]

[Total 3 marks]

Exam Practice Tip

Maintaining biodiversity is generally a good thing — you should know about the positive effects it can have on ecosystems as well as the benefits it can have for humans, such as ecotourism. However, maintaining biodiversity is not always an easy task — make sure you're aware of some of the challenges involved.

Impacts of Environmental Change

Circle either **true** or **false** for the following statements.

Atmospheric gases can affect the temperature of the Earth.   true / false

The distribution of all species tends to stay the
same unless humans cause disruption.   true / false

If water availability in an ecosystem changes, the distribution
of species in that ecosystem may also change.   true / false

1   It is thought that environmental changes in the future will reduce the percentage
     of the Earth's surface that is covered in ice. Explain how this may affect the
     distribution of organisms that are adapted to live on ice, such as polar bears.

....

....

[Total 1 mark]

2   Lichens grow on the bark of trees. They are sensitive to the concentration
     of sulfur dioxide in the air, which is given out in vehicle exhaust gases.
     A road runs by the side of a forest. Scientists recorded the number of lichen
     species growing on trees in the area. The graph below shows the results.

a) How many different species of lichen
    were recorded at 15 m from the main
    road?

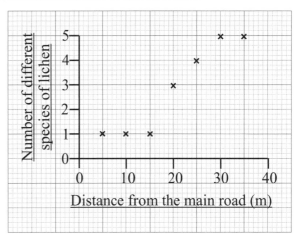

    ....

    [1]

b) Describe the relationship between the
    number of species of lichen growing
    on the bark of trees and the distance
    from the main road. Suggest an
    explanation for your answer.

....

....

[2]

c) Based on these results, what is the minimum distance a road should be
    from a forest to allow at least four species of lichen to grow?

....

[1]

[Total 4 marks]

Topic B6 — Global Challenges

Food Security

1 Which of the following is likely to **negatively** affect food security? (Grade 4-6)

    A   The appearance of a new pathogen of food crops.
    B   People consuming less meat.
    C   The use of drought-resistant crops.
    D   An increased amount of land available for growing crops.

Your answer ☐

[Total 1 mark]

2 Due to the increasing human population size, it is important to develop ways of producing food more sustainably. (Grade 4-6)

What is meant by the term sustainability?

....

....

[Total 1 mark]

3 Human activities threaten global food security. (Grade 6-7)

a) The Earth's temperature is increasing as a result of human activities.
Explain **one** reason why this could have a negative effect on food security in the future.

....

....

....

[2]

b) The use of pesticides on crops may lead to the evolution of new pests that are resistant to the pesticide. Explain why this might be a threat to food security.

....

....

[2]

c) Explain how changing diets in wealthier populations can negatively impact global food security.

....

....

....

....

[3]

[Total 7 marks]

Ways of Increasing Agricultural Yields

Fill in the blanks in the following passage using the words on the right. You don't need to use all of the words.

In order to increase agricultural yields, farmers use methods to reduce

the damage done by .... such as insects. For example,

insecticides are a form of .... control which kill insects.

Agricultural yields can also be improved by .... the

number of crop plants which can be grown in a given area of land.

increasing

decreasing

biological

pathogens

chemical

pests

1   Corn earworm is an insect pest of corn plants.   (Grade 4-6)

Which of the following is an example of a biological control
method that could be used to control the corn earworm?

A   Planting corn plants in a greenhouse rather than outdoors.
B   Applying chemicals to deter the corn earworm.
C   Releasing an insect which eats the eggs of the corn earworm.
D   Using new varieties of corn which contain toxins that kill the corn earworm.

Your answer ☐

[Total 1 mark]

2   The diagram below shows a method of growing crops.   (Grade 6-7)

a) What is the name of the method shown in the diagram?

A   hydraulics
B   hydrostatics
C   hydroponics
D   hydroelectrics

Your answer ☐

[1]

nutrient
solution

b) Give **two** reasons why this method may
be useful for increasing agricultural yields.

....

....

....

....

[2]

[Total 3 marks]

3 A farmer was testing the effectiveness of three different fertilisers. He divided one of his fields into three sections and recorded the mass of the harvest from each section in one year. Then he applied a different fertiliser to each section and measured the mass of the harvest in the second year. His results are shown in the table below.

a) Calculate the percentage change in yield for section **C** of the field.

Section of field	Year 1 mass (kg)	Year 2 mass (kg)	% change in yield
A	1100	1320	20
B	1250	1550	24
C	1300	1703	

answer = ...%

[2]

b) Explain how fertilisers affect the yield of crops.

....

....

....

[2]

[Total 4 marks]

4* In the future, it is thought that climate change may lead to an increased risk of drought in some parts of the world. It might also lead to the movement of pests of crop plants, including insects and weeds, into new regions, resulting in losses in agricultural yields.

Explain how genetic techniques may be used to help grow crops in areas where food could potentially become more scarce as a result of climate change.

....

....

....

....

....

....

....

....

....

[Total 6 marks]

Exam Practice Tip

Remember that combinations of different methods may be used to increase food security, so make sure that you are able to write about all of the different ways that farmers and scientists can increase agricultural yields. Also, be prepared to link the ideas to what you already know about why food security is so important.

Selective Breeding

1 Which of the following does **not** describe a potential use of selective breeding? (Grade 4-6)

  A Producing bacteria with the human gene for insulin.
  B Producing pigs with a high meat yield.
  C Creating a new variety of a plant with larger flowers.
  D Producing a crop plant with high grain yield.

  Your answer ☐

  [Total 1 mark]

2 The diagram shows two cobs (**A** and **B**) which were produced from two different corn plants. Cob **B** is the result of selective breeding over many years. (Grade 6-7)

  a) Based on the diagram, suggest a desirable characteristic of corn plants.

  ....

  [1]

kernels

  b) Explain how this selective breeding process may help with food security.

  ....

  ....

  [1]

  [Total 2 marks]

  A   **B**

3 Due to natural variation some dairy cows in a herd produce a higher yield of milk per day than others. (Grade 7-9)

  a) Explain how selective breeding can be used to produce a herd with high milk yields.

  ....

  ....

  ....

  ....

  [3]

  b) Suggest a reason why the emergence of an infectious disease, such as bovine tuberculosis, may be more of an issue for a herd of selectively bred cows than a herd that haven't been selectively bred.

  ....

  ....

  ....

  ....

  ....

  [3]

  [Total 6 marks]

☹ ☐   😐 ☐   🙂 ☐

Genetic Engineering

Draw lines to connect each word or phrase on the left with the statement describing it on the right.

restriction enzyme	used to identify genetically engineered cells
resistance marker	cuts DNA open
ligase	transfers DNA into a cell
vector	sticks DNA ends together

1   Vectors are often used in genetic engineering.   *Grade 4-6*

Which of these is an example of a vector used in genetic engineering?

A   a stem cell
B   a plasmid
C   a glucose molecule
D   a protein

Your answer ☐

[Total 1 marks]

2   Genetic engineering can be used to produce genetically modified corn plants.   *Grade 6-7*
These plants are grown in many parts of the world due to their pest resistance.

a) Explain what is meant by genetic engineering.

....

....

[1]

b) Apart from pest resistance, give another example of a beneficial characteristic that could be introduced into a crop by genetic engineering.

....

[1]

c) Give **two** reasons why some people may have concerns about the use of genetically modified crops in agriculture.

....

....

....

....

[2]

[Total 4 marks]

3 There are several stages involved in genetically engineering an organism. **Grade 7-9**

a) Outline how a desired gene would be isolated from an organism and then inserted into a vector.

....

....

....

....

[3]

b) Describe how antibiotic resistance markers can be used to identify bacterial cells that have been genetically engineered.

....

....

....

....

....

[4]

[Total 7 marks]

4 A scientist discovers that she is able to genetically modify hens to produce particular substances in the whites of their eggs. **Grade 7-9**

a) Suggest why the scientist's findings might be useful in treating nutrient deficiency diseases in certain countries.

....

....

[2]

b) Suggest **two** ethical objections that some people may have towards genetically engineering hens in this way.

....

....

....

....

[2]

[Total 4 marks]

Exam Practice Tip

Make sure you know plenty of arguments both for and against genetic engineering, as it's quite an important issue. And don't forget the basic principles of using vectors and enzymes to genetically modify an organism — the techniques may vary a little depending on whether it's an animal/plant etc., but the basic idea is still the same.

Topic B6 — Global Challenges

Health and Disease

1 Most plants and animals will experience disease during their lifetime. (Grade 4-6)

   a) What is meant by the term disease?

   ....

   [1]

   Diseases can be communicable or non-communicable.

   b) i) Describe the characteristics of communicable diseases.

   ....

   ....

   [2]

   ii) Describe the characteristics of non-communicable diseases.

   ....

   ....

   ....

   ....

   [3]

   [Total 6 marks]

2 There is often interaction between different diseases. (Grade 6-7)

   a) Patients infected with HIV have an increased probability of developing tuberculosis.
      Explain why this is the case.

   ....

   ....

   ....

   ....

   [2]

   Girls between the ages of 12 and 13 are offered the HPV vaccination.

   b) Explain why this vaccine protects them against cervical cancer.

   ....

   ....

   ....

   [2]

   [Total 4 marks]

Exam Practice Tip

Make sure that you understand the differences between communicable and non-communicable diseases. You might be given information on a disease you don't know about in the exam and asked to work out which category it fits into.

How Disease Spreads

Draw lines to match up each word on the left to the correct description on the right.

Viruses	These pathogens are eukaryotic and usually single-celled. Many of the pathogens in this category are parasites.
Protists	Some of these pathogens are single-celled, while others have a body made up of hyphae.
Fungi	These pathogens are not cells. They replicate themselves inside the infected organism's cells.
Bacteria	These pathogens are prokaryotic, reproduce rapidly and produce toxins that damage your cells and tissues, making you feel ill.

1   Different types of pathogen can cause disease in plants. **(Grade 4-6)**

a) What type of pathogen causes barley powdery mildew?

A   a virus
B   a bacterium
C   a fungus
D   a protist

Your answer ☐

[1]

b) Tobacco mosaic virus (TMV) is a plant pathogen. How is it usually spread?

A   in the air
B   through the soil
C   by direct contact
D   by animals eating infected plants

Your answer ☐

[1]

[Total 2 marks]

2   Infection with the bacteria *Agrobacterium tumefaciens* can cause disease in plants. **(Grade 6-7)**

a) Name the plant disease caused by *Agrobacterium tumefaciens*.

....

[1]

b) Describe how infection with *Agrobacterium tumefaciens* affects plants.

....

....

....

....

[3]

[Total 4 marks]

Topic B6 — Global Challenges

3 The tobacco mosaic virus (TMV) is a widespread plant pathogen affecting many plant species.

Grade 6-7

a) Describe the appearance of a plant with TMV.

....

[1]

b) Outline why a plant affected by TMV cannot grow properly.

....

....

[1]

The table shows the mean diameter and mass of fruits from 100 healthy plants and 100 plants infected with TMV.

	Healthy plants	Plants with TMV
Mean diameter of fruit (mm)	50	35
Mean mass of fruit (g)	95	65

c) Describe the effect of TMV on the diameter and mass of fruit produced in the infected plants compared to the healthy plants.

....

....

....

[2]

[Total 4 marks]

4 HIV is a virus that infects humans.

Grade 6-7

a) HIV is spread via bodily fluids. Give **two** ways in which HIV may be transmitted between people.

....

....

[2]

b) Describe the effects of HIV on the body and explain why people with the virus can become less able to cope with other communicable diseases.

....

....

....

....

....

[4]

c) Other than via bodily fluids, give **two** other ways that communicable diseases can be transmitted.

....

[2]

[Total 8 marks]

Topic B6 — Global Challenges

Reducing and Preventing the Spread of Disease

1   Influenza is a common communicable disease. It is caused by a virus that can be spread by airborne droplets when an infected person coughs or sneezes.

   Grade 6-7

a) Give **two** ways in which the spread of influenza could be reduced or prevented.

....

....

                                                                                [2]

b) Aspects of a person's lifestyle can increase the chance of them developing a communicable disease. Suggest and explain **two** social or economic factors that could also increase the chance of developing a communicable disease.

....

....

....

....

                                                                                [4]

[Total 6 marks]

2   Crop plants are a vital food source for humans. Large scale infection of crop plants could risk the security of the human food supply. Chemical and biological control are two methods that are used to control the spread of disease in plants.

   Grade 6-7

a) Give **one** example of a chemical control method that could be used to control plant disease.

....

                                                                                [1]

b) Apart from chemical and biological control methods, state and explain **two** other methods for controlling plant diseases.

....

....

....

....

....

                                                                                [4]

[Total 5 marks]

Exam Practice Tip

There are quite a few different methods for controlling the spread of plant diseases and those for controlling animal diseases. Make sure you've got a good grasp of them — you might be asked to give examples in an exam.

Topic B6 — Global Challenges

Detecting Plant Disease and Plant Defences

1 A farmer suspects that some of the plants in his crop have a disease. **Grade 6-7**

a) Put ticks next to **two** methods of detecting the disease in the field.

examine the colouring of the leaves of the plants	
detect the presence of antigens in a sample of plant tissue	
examine the roots of the plants	
detect the presence of a substance released by pathogens, using antibodies	

[2]

b) The farmer sends a sample of one of his plants to a laboratory for analysis. Outline how the DNA in the sample could be analysed to identify the presence of a particular pathogen.

....

....

....

[2]

[Total 4 marks]

2 The diagram on the right shows a cross section through a leaf. **Grade 6-7**

a) Explain how a waxy cuticle can defend plants against pathogens.

....

....

....

....

....

waxy cuticle

top of leaf

bottom of leaf

[2]

b) Explain **one** physical defence against pathogens used by individual plant cells.

....

....

....

....

[2]

c) In addition to physical defences, plants are able to use chemical defences. Give **one** way in which these chemicals defend plants against pathogens.

....

[1]

[Total 6 marks]

Topic B6 — Global Challenges

The Human Immune System

1   The body has many features that protect it against pathogens.   (Grade 4-6)

   a)   Describe how the skin helps to defend the body against pathogens.

....

....

                                                                      [2]

   b)   How do structures in the nose help to defend the body against the entry of pathogens?

....

....

                                                                      [1]

                                                          [Total 3 marks]

2*   Describe how the human body works to defend itself against pathogens that have entered the body. Include details of the body's internal defences and the role of the immune system.   (Grade 7-9)

....

....

....

....

....

....

....

....

....

....

....

....

....

                                                                       [Total 6 marks]

Exam Practice Tip

Think carefully about 6 mark questions like the one on this page. Don't just start scribbling everything you know about the topic. Stop and think first — work out what the question is asking you to write about, and then make sure you write enough points to bag yourself as many marks as possible. Good job you've got some practice on this page.

  ☐   ☐   ☐   **Topic B6 — Global Challenges**

Vaccines and Medicines

Use the words below to correctly fill in the gaps in the passage.
You don't have to use every word, but each word can only be used once.

active   white   immune   antiviral   pathogenic
antigens   inactive   memory   vaccines   red

When a person is vaccinated, they are exposed to dead, ... or weakened

pathogens. These are harmless to the body, but carry ...., which trigger an

.... response. .... blood cells produce antibodies to attack

the pathogens. Some of these blood cells remain in the blood as .... cells.

---

1   Which of the following substances can be used to treat a bacterial infection?   *(Grade 4-6)*

   A   antibiotic
   B   antiviral
   C   antiseptic
   D   antigen

   Your answer [   ]

   [Total 1 mark]

2   A boy falls and cuts his leg while running.   *(Grade 6-7)*

   What type of medicine should he apply to his leg? Explain your answer.

   ....

   ....

   ....

   [Total 3 marks]

3   A large proportion of a population is vaccinated against the pathogen which causes mumps.   *(Grade 6-7)*

   a) If the mumps pathogen enters the body of someone who has had the mumps vaccination,
   why would they be unlikely to become ill with mumps?

   ....

   [1]

   b) Explain how vaccinating a large proportion of a population against a disease can help protect
   people from catching the disease who haven't been vaccinated.

   ....

   ....

   ....

   [2]

   [Total 3 marks]

Investigating Antimicrobials PRACTICAL

1 A scientist carried out an investigation into the effects of two different antibiotics (**A** and **B**) on two different cultures of the bacteria *Staphylococcus aureus* (culture **1** and **2**). Separate agar plates were inoculated with each bacterial culture. Three paper discs were then placed on the surface of each plate: one soaked in antibiotic **A**, one soaked in antibiotic **B** and one control disc soaked in sterile water. The agar plates were then incubated for two days to allow the bacteria to grow. The diagram below shows the results of the experiment.

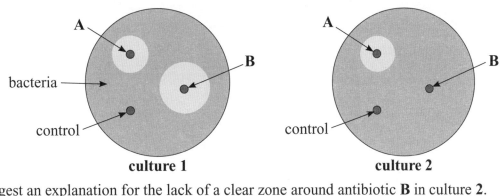

a) Suggest an explanation for the lack of a clear zone around antibiotic **B** in culture **2**.

....

....
[2]

b) Explain why the clear zone around antibiotic **B** in culture **1** is larger than the clear zone around antibiotic **A** in culture **1**.

....

....
[2]

c) Explain why a control disc was used.

....

....
[1]

Aseptic techniques were used when carrying out this investigation.

d) i) Why are aseptic techniques used?

....
[1]

ii) Give **two** aseptic techniques that should have been used during this investigation.

....

....

....

....
[2]

[Total 8 marks]

Topic B6 — Global Challenges

PRACTICAL | **Comparing Antimicrobials**

1   A scientist was investigating the effects of four different antibiotics (**A**, **B**, **C**, **D**)
    on the growth of a bacterial species. She soaked a separate paper disc in each
    antibiotic and placed them on the surface of an agar plate that had been inoculated
    with the bacteria. She also placed a control disc on the surface of the plate. The
    results are shown in the diagram below along with the diameter of each clear zone.

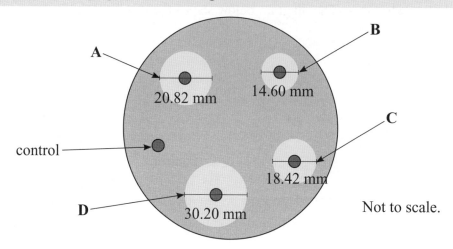

a) Calculate the difference between the areas of the clear zones around
   antibiotic **B** and antibiotic **D**.
   area = πr^2
   $\pi = 3.14$

difference = ... mm²

[5]

b) The experiment was repeated three more times. The scientist noticed some variation in the
   diameter of the clear zone around antibiotic **C**. The table below shows the diameter of this
   clear zone on each of the four plates.

Plate	1	2	3	4
Diameter of clear zone **C** (mm)	18.42	6.85	17.98	18.75

i) Calculate the mean diameter of the clear zone around antibiotic **C** for all four plates.

mean diameter of clear zone **C** = ... mm

[1]

ii) Suggest an explanation for the result on plate **2**.

....

[1]

[Total 7 marks]

┌───┐
│ ***Exam Practice Tip***   │
│ Make sure you don't get confused between the radius and the diameter when working out the area of a clear zone │
│ — the diameter is the width of the circle going through its centre point, and the radius is half the diameter. │
└───┘

Topic B6 — Global Challenges

Developing New Medicines

1 A group of patients are taking part in a double blind clinical trial. **Grade 4-6**

a) Which row (**A-D**) correctly shows which people know who is receiving a placebo?

	Patients	Doctor
A	✓	✓
B	✓	✗
C	✗	✓
D	✗	✗

Your answer ☐

[1]

b) Explain why clinical trials are carried out using a double blind method.

....

....

[1]

[Total 2 marks]

2 Before new drugs are tested on humans, they must successfully pass through a series of initial trials. **Grade 6-7**

a) i) What is the name given to this series of initial trials?

....

[1]

ii) Outline the phases that take place during these initial trials.

....

....

....

[3]

If a new drug successfully makes it through the initial trials, it is then tested on healthy individuals in clinical trials.

b) Explain why the drug is tested on healthy individuals before being tested on people suffering from the illness that it is designed to treat.

....

....

[1]

c) The clinical trial stage of drug testing usually takes place over a very long period of time. Explain why this is the case.

....

....

[2]

[Total 7 marks]

Monoclonal Antibodies

Circle the correct underlined words below, so that each sentence is correct.

Monoclonal antibodies are made by <u>white blood cells</u> / <u>pathogens</u>. They can be used to locate particular pathogens in a blood sample by being bound to a fluorescent <u>dye</u> / <u>drug</u>. The monoclonal antibodies will <u>attach to</u> / <u>kill</u> the pathogen and can be detected.

1   Which of the following statements about monoclonal antibodies are correct?   **Grade 4-6**

a)   Monoclonal antibodies are:

    A   identical to each other and bind specifically to one type of antigen.
    B   different to each other and will bind to different types of antigen.
    C   identical to each other and will bind to different types of antigen.
    D   different to each other and bind specifically to one type of antigen.

Your answer ☐   *[1]*

b)   Monoclonal antibodies are:

    A   produced by hormones.
    B   attacked by the immune system.
    C   extracted from bacterial cultures.
    D   produced from lots of clones of a single cell.

Your answer ☐   *[1]*

[Total 2 marks]

2   Monoclonal antibodies are engineered by scientists.   **Grade 6-7**

a)   During the production of monoclonal antibodies, scientists use antibody-producing cells from animals such as mice. Explain why they must first inject the animal with an antigen.

....

....

....

[2]

b)   During the next stage of monoclonal antibody production, an antibody-producing cell and a tumour cell are fused to produce a hybridoma cell.
Explain why a tumour cell is used to produce the new type of cell.

....

....

....

....

[3]

[Total 5 marks]

3 Monoclonal antibodies have many medical applications, including in the diagnosis and treatment of cancer.

Grade **6-7**

a) Explain how radioactively-labelled monoclonal antibodies can be used to diagnose cancer.

....

....

....

....

....

....

[4]

b) Explain why it is advantageous to use monoclonal antibodies over other forms of cancer treatment, such as normal chemotherapy and radiotherapy treatments.

....

....

....

....

[2]

[Total 6 marks]

4 During pregnancy a woman begins to produce hCG hormone, which becomes present in her urine. The diagram below shows a pregnancy test that uses monoclonal antibodies to detect this specific hormone.

Grade **7-9**

Blue beads with antibodies attached.

Antibody attached to strip.

Not to scale.

Test strip

Explain how this test can show if the hCG hormone is present in a woman's urine.

....

....

....

....

....

[Total 4 marks]

Topic B6 — Global Challenges

Non-Communicable Diseases

For each of the following statements, circle whether the statement is **true** or **false**.

All non-communicable diseases are
more common in developing countries.   true / false

Smoking is a risk factor for multiple diseases.   true / false

Risk factors are always more closely associated
with low incomes than high incomes.   true / false

1   Non-communicable diseases are not spread by pathogens,   Grade 4-6
    instead they are associated with risk factors.

a) Describe what is meant by a 'risk factor' for a disease.

    ....

    ....
                                                                                                            [1]

b) Give **one** risk factor associated with liver disease.

    ....
                                                                                                            [1]

c) Risk factors may be related to a person's lifestyle.
   Which of the following is **not** a lifestyle factor which may be associated with disease?

   A   a person's sleeping patterns
   B   the number of miles walked per week
   C   the presence of a particular combination of alleles in a person's genome
   D   the amount of calories consumed per day

   Your answer ☐
                                                                                                            [1]
                                                                                                   [Total 3 marks]

2   Cigarettes contain tar, which is a substance containing carcinogens.   Grade 6-7
    Carcinogens can cause changes to occur within cells.

a) Explain why smoking is a risk factor associated with cancer.

    ....

    ....
                                                                                                            [2]

b) Apart from smoking, give **one** additional risk factor which may be associated with cancer.

    ....
                                                                                                            [1]
                                                                                                   [Total 3 marks]

3 Some non-communicable diseases are associated with nutrition. For example, kwashiorkor is associated with a lack of sufficient protein in the diet. It is mostly found in developing countries. *(Grade 6-7)*

a) Suggest an explanation for the distribution of kwashiorkor at a global level.

....

....

[1]

b) Whether a person develops diabetes can be linked to their diet. Explain why an increased consumption of foods that are high in fat might lead to a higher incidence of type 2 diabetes.

....

....

....

[2]

[Total 3 marks]

4 A BMI (Body Mass Index) can be used to determine if a person is overweight or underweight. BMI is calculated by dividing a person's body mass by their height squared. *(Grade 6-7)*

This table shows the weight descriptions associated with different BMI values.

Body Mass Index	Weight Description
below 18.5	underweight
18.5 - 24.9	normal
25 - 29.9	overweight
30 - 40	moderately obese
above 40	severely obese

This table shows the BMI values of five patients at a health centre.

Patient	BMI
A	19.2
B	26.1
C	25.3
D	23.8
E	30.6

a) Obesity is a risk factor for cardiovascular disease. Using the information in the tables, suggest and explain which patient (**A-E**) is most likely to be at risk of developing cardiovascular disease.

....

....

[2]

b) Explain why you can't judge whether or not a person will develop cardiovascular disease based on their BMI value alone.

....

....

[1]

c) Apart from obesity, give **two** additional lifestyle factors associated with cardiovascular disease.

....

[2]

[Total 5 marks]

Topic B6 — Global Challenges

Treating Cardiovascular Disease

Use the correct words to fill in the gaps in the passage. Not all of them will be used.

pulmonary vein   blood vessels   asthma   atheromas   blood flow   cystic fibrosis

coronary arteries   toxins   fatty material   aorta   coronary heart disease

Cardiovascular disease is a term used to describe diseases of the .... and

heart. .... is an example of a cardiovascular disease which is caused by

narrowing of the .... due to the build-up of ....

on the inside wall. These deposits harden to form ...., which can restrict

.... to the heart.

1 Doctors were assessing the heart of a patient who had recently suffered from a heart attack. They noticed that one of the main arteries supplying the heart muscle was narrowed. *(Grade 6-7)*

a) Give **two** pieces of lifestyle advice the doctors may give to the patient.

....

....

[2]

b) The doctors tell the patient he could have a surgical procedure to reduce the chance of having another heart attack.

   i) Explain how a surgical procedure could improve the patient's condition.

   ....

   ....

   [2]

   ii) If the patient decides to go ahead with surgery, suggest **two** risks he should be made aware of.

   ....

   ....

   [2]

c) Suggest **two** types of medication that the patient may be prescribed to improve his condition. Describe what each medication does.

....

....

....

....

[4]

[Total 10 marks]

Topic B6 — Global Challenges

Stem Cells in Medicine

1   Which of the following best describes stem cells?   (Grade 4-6)

     A   A stem cell is any type of cell.
     B   Stem cells can develop into different types of cell.
     C   Stem cells are only found in embryos.
     D   Stem cells are very dangerous.

Your answer ☐

[Total 1 mark]

2   Treatments using embryonic stem cells may be able to cure many diseases. However, the use of embryonic stem cells in research and medicine is a controversial subject. Many governments around the world strictly regulate how they are used by scientists.   (Grade 6-7)

a) It is hoped that stem cell treatment could be used in the future to treat patients with spinal injuries.   Explain why embryonic stem cells have the potential to be used in the treatment of a patient paralysed by damage to cells in their spinal cord.

....

....

[2]

b) Lots of research is needed to overcome the challenges presented by using embryonic stem cells in medicine. Suggest a potential medical issue with the treatment suggested in part a).

....

....

[2]

c) Scientists are currently investigating the possibility of using adult stem cells from the patient's own body in some stem cell treatments. Suggest how using cells from the patient's own body may increase the success of stem cell treatments.

....

[1]

d) Give **one** reason why some people are against using embryonic stem cells.

....

....

....

....

[2]

[Total 7 marks]

Exam Practice Tip

Make sure you remember the differences between adult and embryonic stem cells. They each have their own characteristics, which you need to get clear in your head and learn so that you can get them down in the exam.

 ☐   ☐   ☐

Topic B6 — Global Challenges

Using Genome Research in Medicine

1 The Human Genome Project was a major research programme that identified all the genes found in human DNA.   Grade 7-9

a)* Explain the potential importance of research into the human genome for medicine.

....

....

....

....

....

....

....

....

....

....

....

....

....

....

....

[6]

b) There are ethical and practical issues associated with the application of gene technology in medicine. Describe **two** potential issues of using gene technology in medicine.

....

....

....

....

....

[2]

[Total 8 marks]

Topic B6 — Global Challenges

Mixed Questions

1   Alcohol is metabolised in the liver using alcohol dehydrogenase enzymes.   (Grade 4-6)

a) One of the functions of the liver is to break down excess amino acids.

i) Which of the following molecules is made up of amino acids?

A   a carbohydrate
B   a protein
C   a lipid
D   glycerol

Your answer ☐

[1]

ii) What word is used to describe a molecule that is made up of smaller repeating units, such as amino acids?

....

[1]

b) Which of the following sentences about enzymes is **true**?

A   Enzymes speed up chemical reactions in living organisms.
B   Enzymes are used up in chemical reactions.
C   Enzymes are products of digestion.
D   Enzymes are the building blocks of all living organisms.

Your answer ☐

[1]

c) A scientist was investigating the effect of pH on the rate of activity of alcohol dehydrogenase. The graph below shows his results.

i) What is the optimum pH for the enzyme?

....

[1]

ii) Suggest and explain the effect an acid with a pH of 1 would have on the enzyme.

....

....

....

[3]

d) Which of the following statements about alcohol is **false**?

    A   High alcohol consumption can cause liver disease.

    B   High alcohol consumption is a risk factor for cancer.

    C   High alcohol consumption decreases blood pressure.

    D   High alcohol consumption can lead to heart disease.

Your answer ☐

[1]

[Total 8 marks]

2   The diagram below shows a plant cell with one of its sub-cellular structures magnified. The overall movement of four molecules into and out of the sub-cellular structure are also shown.

    Grade 4-6

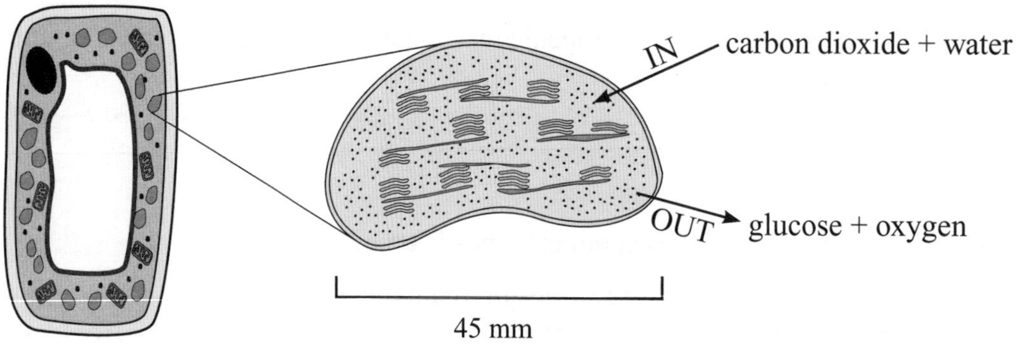

IN — carbon dioxide + water

OUT → glucose + oxygen

45 mm

a) i) Look at the movements of carbon dioxide, water, glucose and oxygen in the diagram. What reaction do these movements suggest is taking place in the magnified sub-cellular structure?

....

[1]

ii) What is the name of the magnified sub-cellular structure in the diagram above?

....

[1]

b) The width of the sub-cellular structure when viewed using a microscope is 45 mm. What is the width of the magnified image in μm?

    A   4.5 μm

    B   0.045 μm

    C   45 000 μm

    D   4500 μm

Your answer ☐

[1]

c) The cell in the diagram is from a leaf.

i) Describe how carbon dioxide enters a leaf.

....

....

[2]

Mixed Questions

ii) What is the name of the process which transports water up a plant and into the leaves?

....

[1]

d) After glucose has been produced by a plant cell, some of it leaves the cell to be transported around the plant. What is the name of the transportation process?

....

[1]

[Total 7 marks]

3 The diagram below shows an example of a woodland food chain. (Grade 4-6)

green plants   ⟶   greenflies   ⟶   blue tits   ⟶   sparrow hawk

a) What term would be used to describe the green plants' position in the food chain above?

....

[1]

b) The diagram below represents a pyramid of biomass for this woodland food chain.
Write the name of each organism in the food chain on the correct level of the pyramid.

←..

←..

....

....

[1]

c) Give **one** biotic factor and **one** abiotic factor that may reduce the amount of green plants in this woodland food chain.

Biotic: ....

Abiotic: ....

[2]

d) Blue tits are also eaten by weasels. Explain what might happen to the population of sparrow hawks if weasels were introduced into the woodland ecosystem?

....

....

....

[2]

[Total 6 marks]

4   Aerobic respiration transfers energy from glucose.

a) i) Name the sub-cellular structures where aerobic respiration takes place.

....

[1]

ii) What would you expect to happen to the carbon dioxide concentration in a person's blood if their rate of respiration increased? Explain your answer.

....

....

....

[2]

b) Glucose is obtained through the diet in animals.

i) Once it has passed through the digestive system, glucose is transported around the body in the blood. Name the liquid component of blood.

....

[1]

ii) Some of the excess glucose from the diet is converted into glycogen and stored in the liver. Explain what happens to this glycogen if the blood glucose concentration falls below normal.

....

....

[2]

c) Plants can store excess glucose as starch.
Describe a test that can be used to identify the presence of starch in a sample.

....

....

[2]

d) Cells respire anaerobically when they cannot get enough oxygen.
During anaerobic respiration, glucose is only partially broken down.

i) Name the substance that is produced during anaerobic respiration in animals.

....

[1]

ii) Give an example of a situation in which a plant's cells may respire anaerobically.

....

[1]

[Total 10 marks]

Mixed Questions

5 Crops can be genetically modified so that they produce substances that they wouldn't normally. An example of this is Golden Rice™. Read the information about Golden Rice™ below.

> Golden Rice™ is a variety of rice that has been genetically modified to produce beta-carotene. Beta-carotene is used in the body to produce vitamin A.
>
> Vitamin A deficiency is a major health problem in some developing countries because many people struggle to get enough beta-carotene and vitamin A in their diet. Golden Rice™ could be used in these countries to help tackle vitamin A deficiency.
>
> Golden Rice™ was genetically engineered using a rice plant, a gene from a maize plant and a gene from a soil bacterium.

a) Explain whether vitamin A deficiency is a communicable or non-communicable disease.

....

....

[1]

b) Explain why the genome of Golden Rice™ will be different to the genome of normal rice.

....

....

[1]

c) Describe the process that may have been used to produce Golden Rice™.

....

....

....

....

....

....

....

....

[4]

d) Genetically modified crops can be useful in helping to improve food security. Suggest **two** ways in which plants could be genetically engineered so that crop yields are increased.

....

....

[2]

[Total 8 marks]

6 In pea plants, seed shape is controlled by a single gene. (Grade 6-7)

The allele for round seed shape is R and the allele for wrinkled seed shape is r.
R is a dominant allele and r is recessive.

a) i) What is the genotype of a pea plant that is homozygous dominant for seed shape?

....

[1]

ii) What is the phenotype of a pea plant that is heterozygous for seed shape?

....

[1]

b) Two pea plants were crossed. All of the offspring produced had the genotype **Rr**.
Construct a genetic diagram to find the genotypes of the parent plants.

Genotypes: .... and ....
[3]

[Total 5 marks]

7 The endocrine system uses hormones to produce effects within the body. (Grade 6-7)
Hormones only affect particular cells, called target cells, in particular places.

a) Briefly explain why target cells only respond to certain hormones.

....

....

[2]

b) State how the speed and effects of a hormone are different to that of a nervous impulse.

....

....

[2]

c) Insulin is a hormone. A person has a mutation in their DNA which causes the structure of
insulin to change. The mutation means that insulin is unable to carry out its normal function.

i) What does insulin control?

....

[1]

ii) Suggest the disease that this person will have as a result of having non-functional insulin.

....

[1]

d) The menstrual cycle is controlled by hormones.

The diagram below shows the change in the levels of these hormones during one menstrual cycle. It also shows the change in the lining of the uterus.

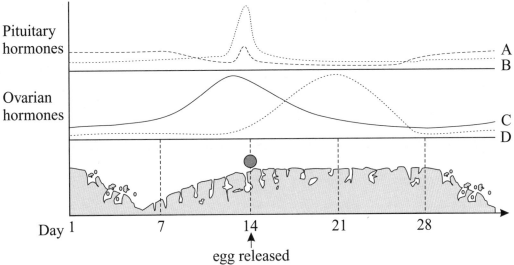

i) Which of the following hormones does line **B** represent in the diagram above.

A LH
B FSH
C Oestrogen
D Progesterone

Your answer ☐

[1]

ii) Which of the following hormones does line **C** represent in the diagram above.

A LH
B FSH
C Oestrogen
D Progesterone

Your answer ☐

[1]

iii) Where in the body is progesterone produced?

....
[1]

iv) Describe how a high progesterone level affects the secretion of hormones from the pituitary gland.

....

....
[2]

[Total 12 marks]

Mixed Questions

8   A farmer selectively bred her tomato plants so they produced larger fruit. Before she
    started the selective breeding process she randomly selected eight tomatoes from her
    original plants (Generation **A**) and recorded their circumferences. She repeated this on
    the plants that were produced several generations later (Generation **X**). Throughout the
    process she controlled all environmental factors that could affect the growth of her plants.
    Her results are shown in the table below.

	Tomato Circumference (cm)								Mean (cm)	Range (cm)
Generation **A**	9.3	13.8	12.5	10.6	12.7	15.4	14.3	13.0	12.7	6.1
Generation **X**	18.2	17.4	16.8	15.6	18.1	17.6	17.2	15.9	17.1	2.6

a) i) Explain why the range of the circumferences is smaller in Generation **X** than in Generation **A**.

    ....

    ....

    ....
                                                                                                                                                    [2]

   ii) Calculate the percentage change in mean tomato circumference between Generation **A**
       and Generation **X**.

                                                                                                                            ....%
                                                                                                                                         [2]

b) The farmer added fertiliser to the soil that she grew her plants in.
    Explain how fertiliser can help a plant to make proteins.

    ....

    ....
                                                                                                                                                    [2]

c) The farmer's tomato plants are affected by aphids, an insect pest.

    i) Suggest **one** method of chemical control which she could use to get rid of the aphids.

        ....
                                                                                                                                                [1]

   ii) Suggest **one** method of biological control which she could use to get rid of the aphids.

        ....
                                                                                                                                                [1]

d) The farmer is considering using hydroponics to increase the yield of her tomato plants.
    Suggest **two** disadvantages of using hydroponics as a method for increasing yields.

    ....

    ....
                                                                                                                                                    [2]
                                                                                                                            [Total 10 marks]

Mixed Questions

9   Many different plant growth hormones are involved in the growth and development of a plant. The diagram below shows the early stages of development of a seed.

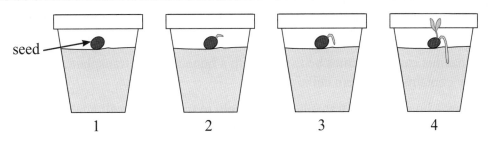

a) i)   What is the name of the developmental process shown in the diagram above?

....

[1]

ii) Name **one** plant hormone which can be used commercially to start this process in some seeds.

....

[1]

b) i)   Which additional hormone is likely to be involved in **stage 4**? Explain your answer.

....

....

[2]

ii) Give **one** commercial use of this hormone.

....

[1]

c)   As the plant continues to develop, the cuticles on its leaves thicken. Use this information to suggest why the plant may be more susceptible to communicable diseases while it is young, rather than when it is mature.

....

....

....

[3]

[Total 8 marks]

10   Sickle cell anaemia is a genetic disorder caused by homozygous recessive alleles. The disorder affects the shape and structure of red blood cells, so they lose their flexibility and become sickle-shaped. This can cause the red blood cells to become stuck in the capillaries.

a) David does not suffer from sickle cell anaemia.
    Which of the following genotypes does David **not** have?

A   SS
B   Ss
C   sS
D   ss

Your answer ☐

[1]

Mixed Questions

b) What aspect of the capillaries' structure makes sickle-shaped red blood cells more likely to become stuck in them rather than in arteries and veins?

....

[1]

c) Sickle cell anaemia can sometimes be treated with a bone marrow transplant.
Bone marrow contains adult stem cells.

   i) Explain how a bone marrow transplant could help to treat sickle cell anaemia.

   ....

   ....

   ....

   [2]

   ii) Scientists think it may be possible to extract stem cells from a patient with sickle cell anaemia, genetically modify them, and then transplant the genetically modified cells back into the patient. Suggest **one** reason why this might be a more effective treatment than a bone marrow transplant from a donor.

   ....

   [1]

   [Total 5 marks]

11 A student was investigating the effect of limiting factors on the rate of photosynthesis by green algae. **PRACTICAL**

The student set up two boiling tubes as shown in the diagram on the right. She also set up a third tube that did not contain any algae. The colour of the indicator solution changes as follows:

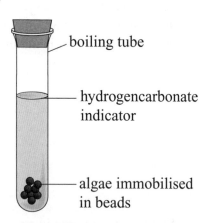

boiling tube

hydrogencarbonate indicator

algae immobilised in beads

- At atmospheric CO_2 concentration, the indicator is red.
- At low CO_2 concentrations, the indicator is purple.
- At high CO_2 concentrations, the indicator is yellow.

The student covered one of the boiling tubes containing algae with foil. All three tubes were left for several hours at room temperature with a constant light source.
The colour of the indicator solution was then recorded.
The results are shown in the table.

	Algae?	Foil?	Indicator colour at start	Indicator colour at end
Tube 1	yes	yes	red	yellow
Tube 2	yes	no	red	purple
Tube 3	no	no	red	red

a) At the end of the experiment, which tube has the highest carbon dioxide concentration?

Tube ....

[1]

Mixed Questions

b) Explain the results seen in Tube **1** and Tube **2**.

....

....

....

....

....

....

....

....

[4]

c) State the limiting factor of photosynthesis that is being investigated in this experiment.

....

[1]

d) Give **two** variables that needed to be controlled in this experiment.

....

....

[2]

A scientist investigating the effect of limiting factors on photosynthesis sketched this graph.

e) What is the limiting factor at point **A**? Explain your answer.

....

....

[2]

f) Name the limiting factor at point **B**.

....

[1]

[Total 11 marks]

12   The life cycle of the protist that causes malaria is shown in the diagram below.

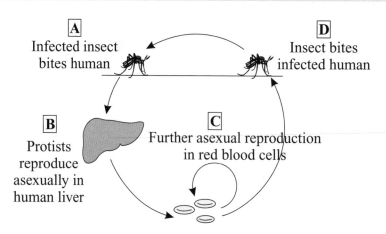

a) Apart from insect vectors, give **one** other mechanism of transmission of communicable diseases.

....

[1]

b) Suggest **one** method of blocking the protist's life cycle at points **A** and **D**.

....

[1]

c) Malaria can be detected in a blood sample using a diagnostic stick which works in a similar way
    to a pregnancy test. The stick is made from a strip of a special type of paper inside a plastic case.
    At one end of the stick, the paper contains antibodies (labelled with dye) that are specific to a
    malaria antigen — this is where a drop of blood and some colourless flushing agent are added.
    A positive result is revealed if a coloured line appears at a point further along the stick, as shown
    in the diagram below.

drop of blood
and flushing   coloured line
agent added here   here indicates a
                        A   **B**   positive result

    i) Suggest why some flushing agent is added with the blood at point **A** on the diagnostic stick.

....

....

[1]

    ii) The sample then moves along the stick. Suggest why a coloured line appears at point **B**.

....

....

....

....

[4]

[Total 7 marks]

BRQ41